EATON GOLF CLUB

1910–2010

EATON GOLF CLUB

1910–2010

Nigel Simpson

Published in Great Britain 2009
by Eaton Golf Club (Norwich) Limited
Newmarket Road, Norwich NR4 6SF
Tel: 01603 451686
Fax: 01603 457539
Email: peter@eatongc.co.uk

ISBN: 978-0-9563107-1-2   Soft-back edition
ISBN: 978-0-9563107-0-5   Hard-back edition

Printed in Great Britain by Barnwell Print Ltd

Front cover:
1920 on 7th green, current 17th, left to right
JM Sampson (Hon Sec/Treasurer)
JH Colman (President)
Geo. Colman
EE Hines (Captain)

Back cover:
Dusk on 14th, taken by Richard Tilbrook.

Frontispiece:
A veteran fourball, combined ages 300,
E Rice, PA Mason, H Giles and WJG Butler.

Contents

7th tee looking back from the green – widely recognised as one of the finest short holes in Norfolk.

Foreword by the Centenary Captain

It gives me great pleasure to congratulate my fellow members of Eaton Golf Club on reaching our Centenary and I extend a warm welcome to all our guests and visitors who will be joining us throughout the year.

I felt honoured and privileged to be asked to serve as the Club's Captain in its Centenary year. I will do my very best to reflect the reputation Eaton has for being both warm and friendly and for embracing the finest traditions of this noble game of golf.

I hope you will find this book engaging, informative and entertaining as its author takes us through the years; you will see that we enjoy a rich heritage and that the special affection our members have for their club is echoed in its pages. For so many members, past and present, our course has been a pasture of joy and wonder.

Our Centenary not only provides us with the opportunity to reflect on the past, but also offers the perfect platform to plan how we should shape

our future. In my view we enjoy an enviable position of being a members' club, in a prime location, which seems to be bucking a local and national trend by maintaining a full membership. We owe a great debt of gratitude to those brave folk who, in 1910, had the vision and determination to create this wonderful club. One hundred years on there could be no more fitting tribute than for us to look forward to the next hundred years; to develop a comprehensive plan which will see us become one of the premier clubs in our region. We should not only maintain a course of the very highest standard possible, but also pursue the development of the new clubhouse that our membership deserves.

I hope you all enjoy the read and I wish you all good golf throughout this very special year.

Colin S Brown

Foreword by the Centenary Ladies Captain

Little did I know when I had my interview as a very nervous novice golfer in 1997 with Elizabeth Clayton, the then Lady Captain, that I would become the Centenary Lady Captain. I feel a great sense of privilege.

Eaton is a wonderful golf club and we have an outstanding Ladies section. I thoroughly enjoyed serving on their committee, especially my two years as Lady Secretary. Our Ladies are highly talented (both on and off the course); enthusiastic, supportive, welcoming and successful.

My family are non-golfers but my husband Mark, a self-professed golf-widower, is looking forward to being my Dennis Thatcher!

I am especially fortunate to have Julia Amey as Lady President. She has given much needed advice and counsel, for which I thank her. By strange coincidence we both attended Peterborough County Grammar School for Girls. We fondly remember our eccentric Headmistress

who taught handwriting to every girl in the school. Those of you who know my writing will realise she failed miserably with me. Thank goodness for computers!

I am looking forward to serving the Ladies Section and Eaton Golf Club in 2010. I hope it will be a year of great golf and good fun.

Catherine Jeffries

Centenary Ladies Captain

Introducing the Author

I am delighted to take this opportunity to
introduce Nigel Simpson, the author of this book.
I have known Nigel since I became a member in
1990. Two things were obvious to me then and
still hold good today: his love for our golf club
and his affection for the members past and
present.

He was born in Judges Walk in 1952 and
joined the club in 1961 following in the footsteps
of his father and maternal grandfather so he has
spent nearly fifty years treading our hallowed
turf. It soon becomes apparent on reading
through the pages of this book that Nigel has
a deep-rooted fondness for Eaton and all it
represents. It was most fitting that he should
be asked to compile this volume, and his hours
and hours of meticulous research have resulted
in a compelling mixture of history and memories.

Nigel was taught to play by the now legendary
Fred Kelly and would often play a few holes on the
way to school at the City of Norwich School (CNS).

He also whiled away the hours helping the Kellys, whipping clubs, cleaning and re-studing shoes, making tea or just having a good old 'mardle'. One of the most enduring truths about Nigel's golf is that it took him nearly 50 years to get his name on the Honours Board, winning the Colman Bowl and Sidney Gill in successive years.

Thank you Nigel, on behalf of the Club and all its members, for all the time and effort that has gone into the production of this book and for 50 years of friendship and good humour.

Colin S Brown

Centenary Captain

Preface

The year is 1910. King George V is crowned in May of this year. Herbert Asquith (Liberal) is starting his second term in office as Prime Minister – in June his government introduces the first old-age pension. William Taft (Republican) is inaugurated as President of the USA and on 20th September, Eaton Golf Club is born.

I felt deeply honoured when asked, some six years ago, to write this 'history' of our club to mark its Centenary. Yet, at the same time, I was somewhat intimidated since John Brister had done such a magnificent job in compiling a record of the first 85 years. Indeed, his research was so painstakingly thorough that very little has been left untold. Therefore my account is, in the most part, a reworking of his information – save the last 15 years.

However, the task has been most rewarding, and I hope that the resulting document is informative, interesting and maybe even enjoyable to those members, past, present and future, who rejoice in this celebration of our club's first 100 years.

Nigel Simpson

The 'tumulus' or burial mound (c4000 BC) situated behind the 10th green

Chronology

50,000 – 10,000 BC
Palaeolithic Era (Stone Age)

In 1943 a flint axe head and antler tools were discovered in the locality near the present 14th green, suggesting that these early hunter-gatherers were probably the first humans to walk the site now occupied by the golf course.

4,000 BC Iron Age

In Victorian times eight 'post-holes' were found on Eaton Heath (now the top part of the course). The purpose of these holes is not certain, but they could have formed part of a wooden 'henge' or ritual ceremonial ground such as the recently discovered 'Sea Henge' at Holme-next-the-Sea. The charred remains of one of these posts have subsequently been radiocarbon dated to c4,000 BC.

2,000 BC Bronze Age

There were originally four 'tumuli', or burial mounds, forming a vast circle on the upper section of the course. One was flattened sometime in the past yet three remain. Two of these are entire, one

View of lower course c. 1920 from current 3rd tee

to the rear of the 10th green, the other at the far end of the practice ground from the clubhouse. The third, much reduced in size, is visible half way down the 18th fairway. One can assume from this

layout that the fourth was probably located half way down the 10th fairway near the cross-bunkers. Each mound would have originally contained one body only. Over the years many Bronze Age weapons and tools have been unearthed, suggesting a sizeable community in the area. Similarly one may assume that Eaton Heath would have been cultivated and used for grazing stock.

Opposite: 18th fairway today with much reduced Bronze Age 'tumulus' or 'round barrow' (middle left).

Below: The Hon Sec bunkered at the 16th. This is the current 18th played in reverse with the 'tumulus' at the rear of the practice ground clearly visible on the left.

1086 Norman England

An entry in the Domesday Book mentions that the heath and Manor of Eaton (then spelled 'Easton') were held by one Eric of Laxfield. The area was defined as being 'two ploughshares'. A 'ploughshare' was the area of land that could be ploughed in one day by one man with one plough and one ox.

1205

The Prior of Norwich Cathedral, who then controlled the Heath as part of the Town Close Estate, granted grazing rights on the land at a cost of one penny per year for each ox or cow or for five sheep.

1806

The *Norwich Mercury* of 7th June advertised for sale

> *A farm at Eaton, chiefly in the occupation of Mr Rice Wicks, comprising an excellent dwelling house, a lime kiln in full operation with three cottages, 330 acres of arable and 60 acres of meadow leasehold to the Dean and Chapter of Norwich Cathedral.*

This farm was located near the present 5th green, as can clearly be seen in the photograph taken in 1921.

Opposite: View from 'Spion Kop' (current 6th green) towards 5th green showing the farm and Lime Kiln Cottages that housed the lime workers for the pits in Danby woods until the early 40's. The photo was taken in the early 1920s.

Below: 'Spion Kop' from the 14th green (looking from the current 7th green towards the 5th). It is worth noting the very open aspect, the hedgerow which would divide the current 4th and 5th holes and the Greenkeeper making use of the state of the art technology of the day!

1849

The Royal Agricultural Show took place on the top part of the course. A well sunk by the small tumulus on the 18th fairway was used as the irrigation source for the first golf course.

c1900

Polo was being played on the land by cavalry officers whose base was in Barrack Street. One of the players was local resident and businessman RJ (Jack) Read.

View from current 7th tee across the 'valley'. It is worth noting the very open landscape of the top part of the course.

1910 The year it all began

In February a public meeting was held, inviting persons interested in starting a golf course in the locality to attend. A committee was elected to 'procure a suitable course and to discuss other details'. The members of that committee were CT Coller, GE Woolsey and RJ (Jack) Read (of the flour milling dynasty).

On 20th September the three-man committee reported back to another public gathering. Jack Read submitted a draft lease on 40 acres he had negotiated with Mr John Gurney of Keswick Hall (Gurneys Bank later merged with Barclays). The lease was to run for seven years at an annual rent of £30; there was to be no play on Sundays and any 'damage' to the land was to be made good (one can only imagine what that meant!). Jack Read reassured the meeting that the lease was very likely to be renewable after the initial term. The original sub-committee had all agreed that until such time as sufficient funds were available there could be no development; subsequent to issuing 100 circulars 67 replies had been received from people anxious to join and £150 had been promised in 'subscriptions'; it was therefore confirmed that the 'Club' was now in existence.

RJ 'Jack' Read the founding father of Eaton Golf Club

The first committee was then elected comprising:

Dr EI Watson (who was to become the first Captain), Major Besant and Messrs Ivor Buxton, CT Coller, HT Giles, Campbell Steward, Lincolne Sutton, Harper Smith, Davidson Walker, Godfrey Woolsey, JH Mannall, 'Golden', RW Collison, RJ Read and AF Gentry as Hon Secretary and Treasurer respectively.

Six of the above were founder members of the Royal Norwich Golf Club which had been formed in 1893 on land also owned by the Gurney family. Indeed Campbell Steward was the Secretary at Royal Norwich from its start until 1917. HT Giles, a member at Sheringham, had been County Champion in 1899. RW Collison was the first Captain of Norwich City FC and also played soccer for Switzerland.

After much debate the fees for membership were set at one and one half guineas annual subscription for gentlemen and one guinea for ladies; half a guinea was payable by juniors. There was an entrance fee of one guinea. Certain gentlemen had promised a total

Extract from the EDP 21st September 1910 reporting the meeting that led to the formation of Eaton Golf Club.

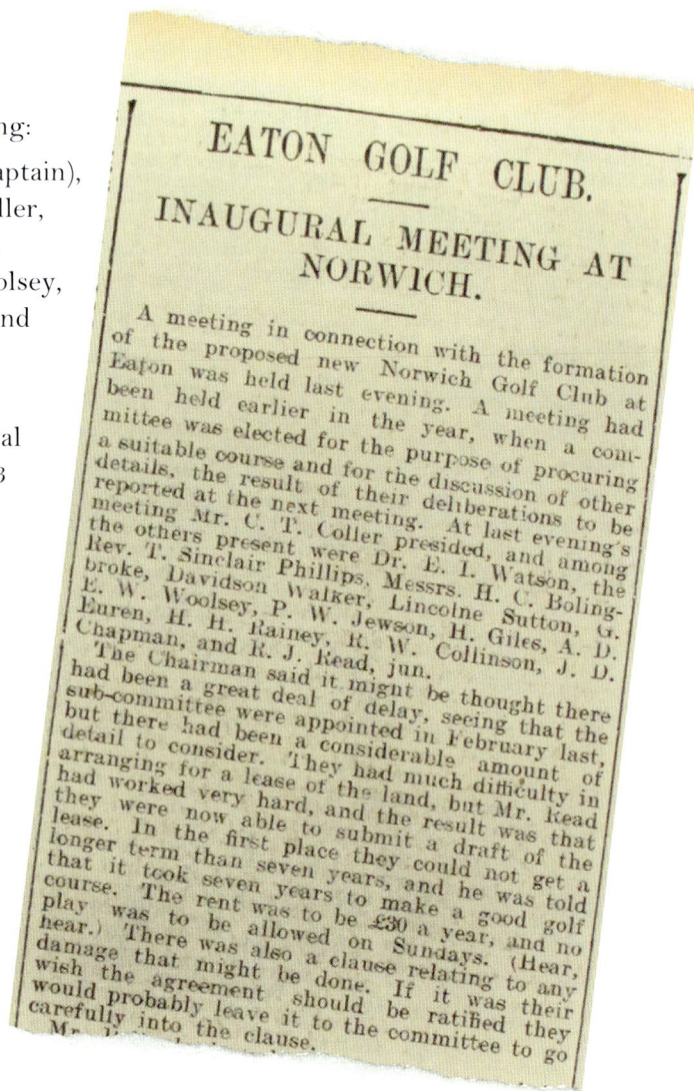

EATON GOLF CLUB.

INAUGURAL MEETING AT NORWICH.

A meeting in connection with the formation of the proposed new Norwich Golf Club at Eaton was held last evening. A meeting had been held earlier in the year, when a committee was elected for the purpose of procuring a suitable course and for the discussion of other details, the result of their deliberations to be reported at the next meeting. At last evening's meeting Mr. C. T. Coller presided, and among the others present were Dr. E. I. Watson, the Rev. T. Sinclair Phillips, Messrs. H. C. Bolingbroke, Davidson Walker, Lincolne Sutton, E. W. Woolsey, P. W. Jewson, H. Giles, A. D. Euren, H. H. Rainey, R. W. Collinson, J. D. Chapman, and R. J. Read, jun.

The Chairman said it might be thought there had been a great deal of delay, seeing that the sub-committee were appointed in February last, but there had been a considerable amount of detail to consider. They had much difficulty in arranging for a lease of the land, but Mr. Read and they had worked very hard, and the result was that they were now able to submit a draft of the lease. In the first place they could not get a longer term than seven years, and he was told that it took seven years to make a good golf course. The rent was to be £30 a year, and no play was to be allowed on Sundays. (Hear, hear.) There was also a clause relating to any damage that might be done. If it was their wish the agreement should be ratified they would probably leave it to the committee to go carefully into the clause.

Mr.

of £150 as previously mentioned, mostly in sums of £5, which it was agreed would be repaid by a 10% reduction in their subscription after the first year until the sum had been cleared. Because of their reduced fees ladies' play was restricted; they were not allowed on the course after 1pm on Thursdays (traditionally half day closing in the city) and Saturdays.

Most interestingly, a fear was expressed that, unless the cost of membership was kept fairly high, the club would become 'inundated with members as the course was so near the city'. It was also

Play on the lower part of the course, 1920s.

agreed that no more than 15 couples should be allowed to play on the course at any one time!

Also present at the meeting was Ernest Riseborough, Professional at Sheringham, who had been invited to give his views as to the viability of the land for the construction of a golf course. In his view the 40 acres available was limited, even for the proposed nine holes, but he felt that 'the land was well adapted to the purpose and would make a sporting course', whatever that might have meant. He was paid the grand sum of £10 per green and a 'quid' a bunker to lay out the links. Sadly no definitive record of those first nine holes remains today. However, it is not unreasonable to

assume that when he designed the first 18 hole course two years later JH Taylor would have left untouched the nine holes which occupied the top part of the course and would have merely added another nine in the valley. Therefore I put forward the theory that the 'original' nine holes could have looked very much like the plan on page 98.

Opposite: A view of the lower part of the course soon after it was opened for play in 1912.

Below: The same view today.

On 11th October the club took possession of the land, and from that point Eaton Golf Club was up and running. Jack Read expected that the ground would be ready for play in about eight weeks, which proved a trifle ambitious since play did not start until June 1911. 11th October is a significant date since it was to be the start of the financial year for the club for many years to come.

Whether by sheer coincidence, or perhaps the news of a new golf club in Norwich had spread fast, the following article appeared in *The Times* for 21st September 1910 in their sporting column:

> *Most golfers have an affection for their home course, sometimes merely a sneaking one, sometimes one that is blatantly patriotic, and even the worst of inland courses look comparatively pleasant in early autumn. Not only does the course look nice, but it is apt to flatter by its easiness. The greens, at any rate after a wet summer, are at their best, and there is plenty of run in the ground. Holes which in the winter are mud and discontent and need two full shots (if heaven grants a good lie) can now be reached with a drive and a mild pitch.*

The 'affection' spoken of has certainly been true of Eaton since its very inception and was abundantly clear in those 'pioneers' of Eaton Golf Club to whom we owe so much today.

Another milestone in the history of the locality which has a close link with that of the Club was that in September 1910 the City of Norwich School, so clearly visible from our present 8th and 9th holes, opened its gates to pupils for the first time. In its early years the school was fee-paying, yet there were many 'scholarship' boys. One such pupil was Cyril 'Inky' Bulman, who was a well-known member of the Club for many years. Indeed 'Inky', who was responsible for helping your author to get his first handicap, was the very first boy to arrive on the first morning, so proud was he to have earned a place and to be wearing the distinctive red cap. His nickname 'Inky' was given to him at the end of that first day because he had never used a pen before, and his teacher apparently observed that there was more ink on him than on the paper!

Above: The current 8th green (3rd on the first course) clearly showing the newly opened City of Norwich School in the background.

Left: The 8th fairway, 1926 looking towards the clubhouse.

The first clubhouse, 1911

1911

The original 'clubhouse' was no more than the corrugated iron shed used by the polo players as a changing room with the addition of a few army huts. It was clearly felt that the facilities were inadequate so a new building was erected at a cost of £108 13s 6d with a further £59 3s 11d spent on furniture and fittings.

NORWICH MERCURY, JUNE 10, 1911.

The new Links of the Eaton Golf Club, Norwich, occupying a pleasant stretch of the land beside Newmarket Road, were formally opened on Tuesday, though play has been obtainable for some months past. The day was devoted to four-ball play between Riseboro (Sheringham) and Sutton (Eaton) as professionals, and Mr BK Wilson (Royal Norwich) and Mr CG Gidney (Oxford University) as amateurs. At the close of the afternoon the latter were the winners. Our photo shows the players 'putting' at one of the greens, the order, from left to right, being Gidney, Riseboro, Sutton, Wilton and G Robertson at the flag.

To celebrate the opening a 'Grand Match' was played on 11th June between W Sutton, the recently appointed first Professional of Eaton, putting, partnered by the designer, Riseborough second left, (Sheringham) and two amateurs, B Knyvet-Wilson (Royal Norwich) and C Gidney (Oxford University). The par, or 'bogey', for those early nine holes was set at 40. Whilst there is no record of scores in the above, the EDP of 18th August reported that on the previous day, while playing with W Bradley, W Sutton (Club Professional) had gone out in 34 strokes and back in 34, total 68 – this representing a score of 12 below bogey.

15

On 31st October a meeting took place at 'Rivington' on Newmarket Road, the home of Mr and Mrs Jack Read. Some 30 lady members attended and Mrs Margaret Davidson-Walker was appointed the first Lady Captain, Miss Ida Bond, Hon Secretary and a five strong committee elected. Ever since then the lady members of Eaton have been responsible for the running of their own affairs.

On 16th November, a Thursday, the first men's club competition was staged. The winner was G Starling whose score for 18 holes was 106 – 24 – 82.

Clearly the Club was now in full swing with around 250 members of whom 93 were ladies who evidently formed an important and integral part of the picture right from the very start.

1912

This year saw three significant events in the history of Eaton Golf Club; firstly, the extension of the course to 18 holes, secondly the appointment of 'Dick' Kelly as Professional in succession to Sutton, and lastly the first AGM.

With such a large and ever-growing membership the need to extend the existing nine holes to a full 18 became self-evident. On 6th February the then Club Captain, Capt LE Gurney suggested that the advice of JH Taylor, the Royal Mid-Surrey Professional and five times Open Champion be sought. He had a widespread reputation as a golf course architect both at home and abroad; one of his more notable layouts being Royal Birkdale.

Taylor formed part of the 'Great Triumvirate' along with Harry Vardon and James Braid; Taylor himself was responsible for setting up the PGA.

He was much impressed by the 'view across the Vale of Keswick and the wooded heights beyond' and felt that Eaton 'should now become quite a first class golf links'. The committee agreed to adopt his plans. No record survives of the 'Taylor' layout, but it can be assumed that it differed little from the course of 1921. Although many of the greens and tees no longer exist the old 3rd green is clearly visible as the depression half way down the now 5th fairway. (The 5th as we play it today was two shorter holes.) See the plan on page 99.

Later in the year 'Jack' Read and Capt Gurney, who was related to the landowners, managed to persuade JH Gurney to lease the Club

PUTTING ONLY

the remaining land on the City side of Marston Lane thus enabling the work to go ahead.

In November of that year R (Dick) Kelly took over the position of Club Professional starting the long association between the Kelly dynasty and Eaton.

No minutes survive of that first AGM held on 8th November but the Statement of Accounts for the year ending 11th October 1912 makes interesting reading. Whilst the Pro, presumably Sutton, was paid £39 for the year, an entry under 'Horse Keep' shows an expenditure of £55 7s 6d. In addition to this the club also paid £9 10s for 'Hire of Horse', indicating the importance of these noble steeds in the construction and maintenance of the course in the pre-tractor era. A further clue to the eminence of the Ladies' Section was that prizes for men's competitions cost a mere £2 2s yet the Ladies' prizes totalled £3 17s 6d.

JH Taylor, five times Open Champion, who was commissioned in 1912 to design the first 18 holes course incorporating the recently acquired land in the valley. He is pictured, seated, with the other members of the Great Triumvirate; Harry Vardon, centre, and James Braid, who designed Royal Norwich.

REPRODUCED BY KIND PERMISSION OF THE ROYAL AND ANCIENT GOLF CLUB OF ST ANDREWS

Bentfield C Hucks and his Bleriot, 'Firefly', in 1912.

One other trivium from 1912 was that the first flight over Norfolk landed on Eaton Common near Church Lane, which equates to the area around our present 16th tee. The pilot, Benfield C Hucks, flying a Bleriot XI monoplane called 'Firefly', had taken off from Gorleston in the early morning, intending to cross the county and to land at King's Lynn. On landing, he was mobbed by enthusiastic crowds demanding his autograph.

1913

It is worth noting at this point that on 12th March the first recorded Ladies Medal took place. Miss Ida Bond won Division 1 with a net 82 playing off 17 handicap. The best overall net score was 76 by Mrs L Grimes playing off 41.

Little golf appears to have been played during the war years, presumably most men were away at war.

The EDP of 5th July 1919 reported that the club now had 18 holes back in play. The report stated that 'although some of the greens are still rough, the course is generally in very fair condition in spite of the drought'. In celebration there was a match played between the Gentlemen and Ladies (won by the former).

1914–1918

THE GREAT WAR

The following members gave their lives in the Great War

SC Barker

FJ Cole

RT Coller

EM Coller

A Randall

LJ Row

1921 The Fire

On Saturday night 28th May the then club-house was totally destroyed by fire. The fire spread rapidly, the structure being mainly of timber and, despite the alarm being raised by residents on Newmarket Road in the early hours and the prompt attendance of the new motor fire pump accompanied by the chief fire officer, the building was very soon razed to the ground. All that could be done was to try to prevent the fire spreading to outbuildings such as Kelly's shop and the stables. The event was of such importance that even the Chief Constable, JH Dain, put in an appearance. The fact that he was a prominent member of the club had nothing to do with it, I'm sure!

The loss of all club records to that point meant that, as previously mentioned, newspaper articles apart, much of the history of the early years was lost. Many members also lost their equipment. Being hickory shafted they were only so much tinder and the following morning several distraught golfers searched the ashes for the remains of their clubs.

In the meantime the Committee met in the open air by Kelly's shop at 6pm to discuss what should be done. Two members of that committee were Sidney Gill,

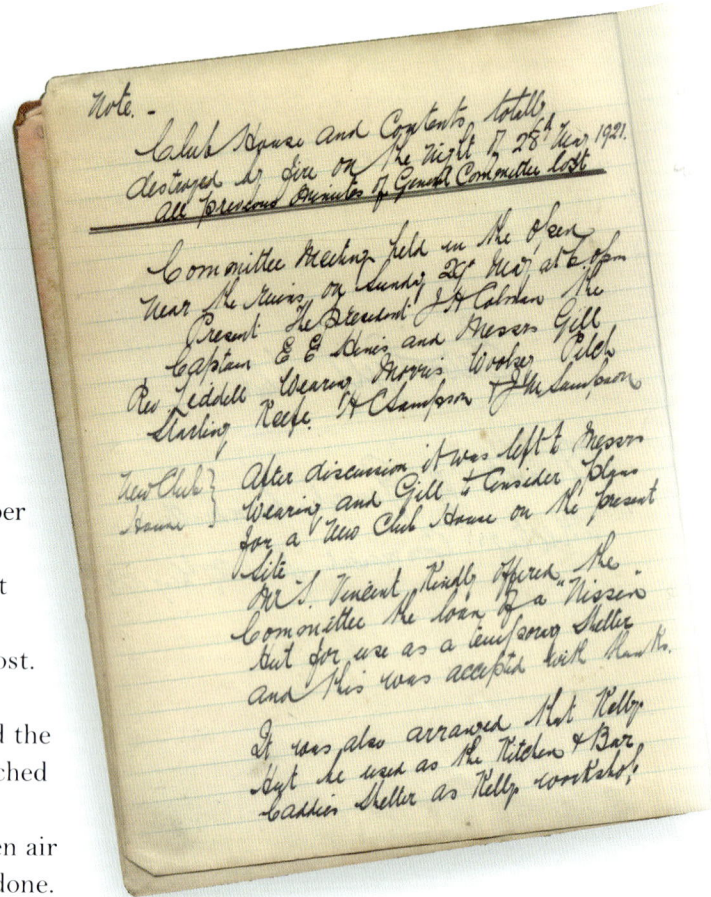

ALL THAT WAS LEFT OF IT.

Ruins of the Eaton Golf Club-house after the fire on Saturday night. Kelly's shop (right corner) had a fortunate escape, considering how close it stood to the scene of the fire.

R. 5.21

Opposite: The earliest surviving club minutes taken the day after the fire of 1921 which destroyed not only the clubhouse but all existing records.

Above: The ruins of the Club-house after the fire. Kelly's shop (right corner) had a fortunate escape, considering how close it stood to the scene of the fire.

the head of the local firm of builders, and Stanley Wearing, the renowned architect and architectural historian. (His book *Beautiful Norfolk Buildings* remains to this day the definitive work on the history of Norfolk architecture.) As the meeting closed these two were assigned the task of designing and building a new clubhouse on the site of the original. In the interim Mr S Vincent offered a 'Nissen Hut' as temporary shelter which was accepted with thanks. Thus began the 50 year association between Mr Gill and his beloved Eaton Golf Club; more of which later.

Twelve weeks later, on 22nd August, the new clubhouse was ready for use. You can see the form of the building as it now comprises the main part of the existing bar/lounge. The pillars by the picture windows were originally outside and supported a canopy over the veranda. Stanley Wearing charged no fee for his design and Sidney Gill undertook the construction at cost. In recognition of their generosity the club presented each with an engraved silver tea service at the opening ceremony on 25th August.

Since most members had lost their equipment in the fire, Professional 'Dick' Kelly and RG Pilch, of the sports shop in Brigg Street, were asked to go to London to purchase clubs that could be sold to members. Kelly was to be paid 5% commission and Pilch would arrange for a salesman to help. Your author is the proud owner of one such club!

Just prior to the fire Ted Ray and George Duncan had played an exhibition match at Eaton. Both were Open Champions, 1912 and 1920 respectively, and Ray was the last Englishman, in 1920, to win the US Open until Tony Jacklin in 1970. In the morning, Duncan scored 72 compared to Ray's 83. In the afternoon they played a match against Dick Kelly and Roy Donald (Royal Norwich) which they won comfortably. One finds it difficult to imagine an Open Champion of our days deigning Eaton worthy of a visit!

1922

Following the erection of the new clubhouse attention then turned to the course itself. Whilst there had been 18 holes for play prior to the Great War, these must have been very 'compact' occupying the land on the clubhouse side of Marston Lane. JH Taylor was once again consulted but would only agree to any alteration if it was adopted in full. However the committee decided that the plan was too costly.

A group outside the 'new' clubhouse at the Ray v Duncan exhition match. JH Colman, President sits front centre.
To his left are Duncan, EE Hines (Captain) and Ray.

Above: 'Foreman' Gaul on the Club's first tractor which finally replaced the horses in 1924.

Opposite: Dick Kelly (middle row 2nd left) played along with his sons Russell and George (front row 3rd and 4th from left).

1923

Sidney Gill successfully negotiated a six year lease to rent 30 acres more land which comprised the area of the Civil Service Sports Ground at the end of Wentworth Green by what was known in my childhood as 'Donkey Lane' and the land adjoining the present car park. The work was undertaken by Corporal EF Gaul MM, the Head Greenkeeper and sub-contracted labour, to a plan drawn up by Sidney Gill, and the new holes were ready for play in April 1925. A noticeable feature of 'Gill' design was the raised banks to the rear of each green still evident on many of today's holes.

Apparently Sidney hated seeing a shot run through the putting surface resulting in an awkward chip back.

No doubt with the purchase of the club's first tractor this year, to replace one of the horses, the task was made somewhat easier. It also made the unfortunate equine incident of 1922 unlikely to reoccur. A horse had been purchased at auction for 20 guineas only to be found to be in foal and therefore unable to work! In 1924 the committee was told that the tractor was working satisfactorily and it was decided to dispose of the remaining horse.

1925

On 15th July the East Region qualifying round of the PGA News of the World tournament was held at Eaton.

PROFESSIONAL GOLFERS AT EATON.

AT EATON GOLF COURSE YESTERDAY 38 PLAYERS COMPETED WITH THE EASTERN SECTION OF THE PROFESSIONAL GOLFERS' ASSOCIATION IN
THE QUALIFYING STAGE OF THE "NEWS OF THE WORLD" TOURNAMENT.
A GROUP TAKEN BEFORE THE START OF THE FIRST ROUND.

1931

After much persuasion Sidney Gill agreed to submit three plans for further development of the course on 31 acres of land on the marsh side of Marston Lane. This land, now occupied by holes 12 to 16, became available on a 20 year lease from John Gurney following an unsuccessful bid to purchase the course and on the proviso that the club surrender the land between the clubhouse and Newmarket Road.

Mr Gill apparently consulted Norwich born Open Champion of 1923 Arthur Havers regarding the layout but the eventual design was primarily Sidney's. The holes differed from their present form in two ways: the short 4th, now 13th, had its green nestling in the hollow to the right of the present 14th tee and the 3rd, now 12th, tee was located in the marshes adding some 40 yards to the present hole. The resulting 18 holes measured 6305 yards in total and represented the course pretty much as we play it today. The new course was officially opened for play on 17th April 1933. In the Club handbook of the early 1950s Tom Scott, a golfing journalist, wrote:

The Club officials could not have put the job in better hands than those of Mr Gill. He had known the course intimately, he had studied golf course architecture and above all he loved Eaton.

One interesting feature however was that the two nines were reversed (i.e. the first tee was immediately outside the clubhouse entrance). This was changed to its familiar format in December 1936.

The cost of constructing these new holes was met by a debenture issue of £700 to members which paid 4% interest p.a. redeemable after ten years.

However the extended course resulted in renewed interest in the club and membership now stood at a very healthy 500. Gentlemen members paid four guineas a year, ladies two and juniors one guinea. There was an entrance fee of six guineas. From the very start the committee realised that Green Fees were an important source of revenue for any golf club. In 1935 those at Eaton were set at three shillings per round for gentlemen and two shillings and six pence for ladies. Interestingly there were weekly and even monthly rates.

Sidney Gill, at the tiller of his blue buggy, pictured by the pine tree adjacent to the 7th green today. Beside him is Alec Crosskill (Captain 1949/50) and in the rear Dr Maxstead and Dr English.

27

22nd July 1936.   House Committee Meeting   5·30 Club. House

Present.   Mr Dain in the Chair. Others Miss Back
Messrs E.E. Hines, F. Green, F.W. Morris & S.J. Wearing

Minutes   The Minutes of the previous Meeting of
April 21st were read. confirmed & signed.

Price List   Owing to the drop in profits on the
catering the prices charged for refreshments
were examined & it was agreed to fix
the prices as follows.

4 Digestive Biscuits	2
Pot of tea each.	4
Tea & Biscuits (assorted)	7
Tea. Bread & Butter	7
" " " & Jam.	9
Tea & Toast	8
" " " (Anchovy)	10
Cup of Coffee	3
Cake.	4
Cheese Sandwiches (4)	6
Ham or Meat "	9

Scones	2
" Toasted	3
Glass of Milk	3
Bread (round) Butter Cheese	6
Soup.	6
Fruit salad	6
Lunches. Meat salad }	2/6
Potatoes . Cheese & biscuits }	

It was decided to leave the prices of drinks
as before, but to try draught Ale &
Pale Indian Ale from Youngs, Crawshay &
Youngs.

Bass Nips.	8½
Lager.	8
Bass, Worthington & Guinness	7
Tolly	6
Cyder. Dry.	6
" Sweet	5
Baby Pollys	3
Schweppes Ginger Beer, Ale, Tonic	5
Caleys " " " "	4
" Small Lemon.	4.

Another indicator of the cost of golf in those days was the bar prices in the late 30's. Above is an extract from 'House Committee' minutes 1936 showing the prices. For the purposes of comparison 12d is equal to 5p today.

——∗◦∗——

1939–45

THE SECOND WORLD WAR

WE SHALL REMEMBER THEM

J Curl

MI Green

G Morris

——∗◦∗——

Obviously the war had a great effect on the lives of many Norwich families, Eaton Golf Club was no exception. Much of the male membership was called up and, apart from those above who made the ultimate sacrifice, several were prisoners of war in camps in Europe and particularly the Far East, where The Norfolk's suffered heavy losses.

Bert Kelly, youngest son of Club Professional Dick, was appointed joint Professional with his father in August 1939. He was reported 'missing in action' in June 1941 but was later confirmed as a prisoner in a camp on the German/Polish border where he remained for the duration of the war.

One poignant pointer to the waste of the nation's youth was that J Curl, who was one of the club's three dead, had won the Ward Junior Cup in 1933 and 1934.

In early 1940 pits were dug on the fairways and the earth removed was placed in piles; similarly oil drums were filled with soil and placed all over the fairways to thwart both enemy glider landings and the advance of German vehicles should the invasion come. Indeed the whole country, following Dunkirk, lived in fear of invasion. Norwich suffered heavily in the Blitz and there was a substantial anti-aircraft gun battery in Eaton village – German bombers would have followed the River Yare on their way to strategic targets such as the Boulton & Paul and Laurence & Scott factories near the railway station. Fred Kelly told me when I was a junior that he used to watch enemy aircraft flying over the course most evenings from the top of the

tumulus by the 10th green. Indeed in the early days of the war a Hawker Hart spotter plane from Duxford airfield crash landed on the 3rd fairway!

A more significant impact on the course was a letter sent to the club in March 1941 by the War Agricultural Committee, who asked that, in the interest of vital food production, the 30 acres on the far side of Marston Lane should be ploughed up and barley planted. As a result, the 10th, 11th, 17th and 18th were played as the opening four holes and then again as the final four. In order to make a full 18 holes the present 5th was split in two. The depression, which can be seen in the middle of the fairway, was a bunker before the green of one hole and there was a tee next to the fourth tee to the present green, a par 4, thus reverting to the layout of 1921. Despite the ploughing up of the fairways over the road the greens continued to be maintained throughout the war.

Another agricultural disruption to the normal running of the club was that local farmer Mr Westgate was allowed to graze his sheep on the course. They were penned in moveable hurdles in order to prevent damage to the greens. They continued to roam the links until 1946.

'Dick' Kelly with Percy Calver Head Greenkeeper in the doorway pictured just prior to World War II.

Stan Calver, now a club member, has many souvenirs of the course in the war years. His father, Percy, was the Greenkeeper at the time and worked alongside Ernie Gaul.

I was a schoolboy at the CNS at the time but I spent much of my holidays working as a 'dogsbody' in the vain hope that it might keep me out of trouble. I was also one of the last caddies, if not the last, to work at the club. I carried Mr Gill's clubs on a Saturday afternoon, they were 'Bobby Jones' make and I had to clean them afterwards with a soft cloth and sand for which I received the princely sum of four shillings! Mr Gill kindly let me play the occasional shot. The other caddy at the time was called 'Chalk Pit Charlie' who worked on the chalk pits in Eaton.

One morning the course was festooned with wire, small parachutes and explosives – an aerial minefield that was supposed to have dropped on German bomber formations in the night. Quite an excitement for a scruffy schoolboy! Later one or two incendiary bombs fell on the course and I excavated the remnants in the soft earth the following day. Similarly, but a little more alarming, a cannon shell pierced the roof of one of the sheds, bounced off a beam and embedded itself in the threshold. I found it one Saturday morning while inspecting a swallow's nest. After much struggling to remove it

I reluctantly had to leave it for another day, only to be thwarted by the Bomb Disposal Squad who removed the entire threshold because it was live and dangerous. I said nothing!

Another morning a drop tank from a German plane was found on the course. Before its removal dad managed to syphon off most of its contents. Mixed with TVO tractor fuel it seemed to work quite well.

There was also a Barrage Balloon Unit camped by the 9th green, near the clubhouse. I still have the Monopoly set they gave my father when they left.

When I asked Stan about the players during the war he said that they were mostly 'old boys' who had done their bit in the 1914–18 conflict. There were also frequent American visitors from nearby airbases who, like serving British troops on leave, were given the courtesy of the course for the duration. One of the American officers, Colonel Michael G Phipps, donated a Trophy, paid for by contributions from fellow airmen, to be played for annually on a date as near as possible to VE Day. The silver salver has an engraving of a Liberator B24 bomber on one side and the letter on page 33 on the reverse.

Major (later Lt Colonel) Michael J Phipps seated 4th from left front row; 2nd left is the famous Holywood star
Col James Stewart. Phipps was Intelligence Officer in the 93rd Bomber Group and the photo was taken in June 1944
just prior to D-Day when he was stationed at Ketteringham Hall, near Hethersett. His major military claim to fame was
planning the low-level bombing raid on the Poelesti oil fields in Romania, a vital supply to the German war machine.

95th Combat Bomb Wing
APO 558
US Army

Dear Sir,

Having received the gratuitous hospitality of the Eaton Golf Club for nearly two years I must take this opportunity to thank you and the club members for your kindness and the many pleasant rounds I have played on your course. I suggested to Mr Kelly that I would regard it as an honour if I might be permitted to give a trophy of some sort for a division of one of your tournaments but, as a governor of a club at home, I am very conscious of the fact that cups are not always the most pressing need. So if the club will do me the honour of accepting it I am enclosing a contribution to be used as your governors see fit with the hope that it may be used in some way which will give your members a small part of the pleasure which I have had as part of a horde of Americans who have overrun your course. I hope that someday under happier circumstances I may have another chance to play a round at Eaton or better still that I may have the opportunity of having some of your members play at my club in Meadow Brook, Westbury, Long Island, NY. Until that time I remain,

Yours Sincerely,

Michael G Phipps (Lt Col AC)

Many of these young aviators were called from the course in mid-round to report to their airfield. They frequently had left valuables in the care of Dick Kelly who returned them on their next visit. Sometimes he had to surrender them to a mournful comrade for the owner had not come back from his mission.

Cyril Ramsay, who joined the club when Earlham closed in 1963, although not a golfer at the time, also has memories of the course in 1940. A local lad, Cyril joined up in June 1940 – a very hot day as he recalls:

We were ordered to report to the Norfolk's barracks on Mousehold yet when we arrived they said they knew nothing about us. We were all young lads in our teens and like the others I was wearing my best suit and was boiling. The roads were dusty and my main concern was my new suit, which was quickly being ruined! We were told to walk down to Thorpe railway station where we were to be met by regulars who would know what to do with us. They then transported us all through the city to Town Close School, on Newmarket Road, where we were to be based. We were issued with bedding

33

and basic uniforms. The blankets we were given must have dated from the First War and I asked the corporal where the sheets were, you can only imagine the mouthful I got. Even when a prisoner in Burma the lads teased me about my 'sheets'. During our basic training we were frequently woken at about 1 am with the call that the Germans had landed and had to run up Newmarket Road to the golf course for night exercises. Our HQ was the mound behind the 10th green and we would spend the night crawling on our bellies through the rough and bushes. When we had finished we marched back to the school. However I knew the area well and would often take a short cut back along Marston Lane and up Ipswich Road. When the lads eventually got back I was lying in my bunk, they never did work out how I beat them home!

1946

The 'over the road holes' reopened for play in early 1946. Following the war, members gradually began to return to golf but the membership had dwindled well below the 500 of the early thirties. At this time Frank Nicholls, a local bank manager and member since 1926, recently demobbed himself, was given the task of recruiting new members. Frank held the offices of Captain (1955), President (1970–71) and was elected an Honorary Life Member for his services to the club. He was playing regularly into his late eighties and always had a welcoming baritone 'Hello' for members and visitors alike. I particularly recall his role as host of countless Christmas parties, where he ran the draw and games with charm and unerring efficiency. It was due to Frank and many others like him that Eaton survived the lean post-war years.

1950s

The era of the fifties was about the most stable in the history of the Club. The membership was fairly constant and the course, which was undoubtedly at its most challenging, was unchanged.

In 1950 an Exhibition Match took place on 7th May between tour professionals Max Faulkner, famed for his plus-twos, and Charlie Ward and club pro Bert Kelly partnering club member and scratch golfer George Pilch. Max Faulkner went on to win the Open Championship the following year at Royal Portrush.

Bert Kelly teeing off the 1st in the Faulkner/Ward exhibition match. Bert's brother and assistant Fred is seated on the shooting stick by the teebox.

Max Faulkner and Charlie Ward on the 9th green. Kelly's shop behind.

Similarly, in 1953 another match was played to raise money for the East Coast Flood Appeal when club pro Bert Kelly teamed up with the Earlham pro Leslie Ball to challenge Reggie Knight, a tour player from Wanstead Golf Club and Eddie Whitcombe from Chigwell Golf Club; £50 was raised.

The reputation of Eaton as a test of golf and a friendly club was spreading far and wide. Indeed a double page centre spread in the January 1953 edition of *Golf Illustrated*, a leading national publication, was glowing in its praise. Under the sub-heading 'Eaton, Norwich, a progressive club with a sporting layout' author Tom Scott went on to describe the course. Although he was unable to play because of the snow he nonetheless drove around the course with Sidney Gill, Cecil Amey and Bert Cann. Afterwards he concluded that

'The surroundings are certainly most beautiful, and the holes have been designed to be both a good test of golf and yet essentially fair'.

His hole-by-hole guide to the course deserves reproduction in full, for it represents an unbiased assessment.

First Hole   455 yards   Par 5
This is a big opening hole and dog-legged to the right just for good measure. The green is rather on the edge of a plateau with a not inconsiderable drop beyond. As there is some danger on the right and bunkers near the green this is anything but a gentle start.

Second Hole   140 yards   Par 3
A charming little hole of the variety that I like, but it is not as simple as it looks. As one would expect, the pitch to the green has to be most accurate.

Third Hole   464 yards   Par 5
Another man-sized hole played from the high part of the course to the valley. The chief point of the hole is the placing of the drive, although the careful siting of the green and protective bunkers make hitting the green a hazardous business. I advise caution at this hole.

Fourth Hole   412 yards   Par 4
There is still little respite as this fine start keeps up the challenge. The correct thing to do here is to hold up the drive to the right, for the ground slopes down to the other side where trouble awaits. Most players will find difficulty in getting home in two here.

Fifth Hole   500 yards   Par 5
The longest hole on the outward half. There is plenty of trouble on both sides of this one with out of bounds all along the right. This is a fine hole and a pretty one too – a good five for anybody for a rash act may well ruin a card.

Sixth Hole   316 yards   Par 4
A good two-shotter and I think the chief problem here is the judging of distance of the second. There is a tendency for many people to be short and the green is well guarded. Incidentally, with this hole we are back again on the plateau.

Seventh Hole   166 yards   Par 3
Here we have an uphill short hole. The green slopes upward too and there are bunkers around; two on the right and a couple cut into the slope on the left. My advice here is to take one more club than first considered.

Eighth Hole   436 yards   Par 4
There are two routes to the green at this hole; one over the trees for the brave and strong and one round the trees for the rest of us. The green is an unusual shape and well guarded by bunkers.

Ninth Hole   330 yards   Par 4

The boundary is on the right of this one so slicers have to be careful. In the main, however, a four should be in the scope of most players.

Tenth Hole   459 yards   Par 5

We are now back close to where we started and we open the second half as we did the first with a really big hole. The menace here is the boundary which is hard to the right all the way and comes even closer as one approaches the green.

Eleventh Hole   361 yards   Par 4

This is a fine hole played from a high tee over a great jungle of gorse in the open country below. If the tee shot is successfully negotiated the hole is fairly straightforward.

Twelfth Hole   366 yards   Par 4

Now we cross a little lane to play the next few holes. The drive is uphill and there are little woods on either side. Here again the drive is of the utmost importance, for a bad tee-shot makes the second, which has to clear some bunkers, very awkward indeed.

Thirteenth Hole   166 yards   Par 3

The green here is not only well bunkered but a sliced shot or one hit too long or slightly hooked can find fearful trouble. A very fine short hole.

Fourteenth Hole   345 yards   Par 4

Down towards the river at this one. There is some clever bunkering and both tee shot and approach must be well struck if sand is to be avoided.

Fifteenth Hole   343 yards   Par 4

We play back uphill at this one. Guardian trees eat into the fairway but the gap is wide enough for all but the wildest hitters. The green is again well protected by sand and one would be well advised to take an extra club on the approach.

Sixteenth Hole   514 yards   Par 5

This is the longest hole on the course, but the fall of the ground is in our favour. For such a hole a good first and second are necessary and there is a diagonal set of bunkers and another near the green which present a real problem. This hole can be a real card spoiler.

In 1954 the inaugural meeting of the Norfolk Alliance took place at Eaton. The Alliance is a society of amateurs accompanied by local professionals who play monthly through the winter season at courses around the county. Bert Kelly putting on the 18th. He is closely watched by his Amateur team mate Mervyn White of Howlett & White shoe manufacturers.

Seventeenth Hole   302 yards   Par 4

This is a left-hand dog-leg round the corner of copse. The green is set into the edge of the plateau, which is such a feature of this course, and has on the left a deep hollow and on the right a spinney. Although the hole is bunker free there is little room for error.

Eighteenth Hole   456 yards   Par 5

This is a fine finishing hole – a sharp dog-leg left played from a tee back among the gorse. I advise some caution here and pity the poor golfer who is trying to pick up a stroke here for I should think it has broken many a heart. The green is well guarded and altogether it provides a fighting finish to a good testing round.

Total yardage   6521   Par 75   SSS 73

Several points are well worth observing about the above. Firstly consider the 'par' of certain holes, namely the 1st, 3rd, 10th and 18th all of which would be rated as par 4's by modern criteria and yet were par 5's. No doubt this reflects the advances in both club and ball technology over the years which have resulted in us all hitting the ball further and sometimes straighter!

One or two holes of the 1950s layout would be unfamiliar to the current crop of players. The tee for the 1st was right beside the 18th green and is still evident. The 6th was played into the far top right corner of the course, now rough ground, over-run by grass and scrub. The short 7th was played from that corner to the now 6th green between the oaks and the pine trees one can still see if looking back from the present

Plain sailing...

For Over a Century this So...
has provided a prompt and eff...
Savings and House Par...
Service

Norwich Buil...
Society

ST. ANDREW'S HOUSE, NO...

Telephone 21367

Member of the Building Society...

C. E. GARDNER

70 QUEEN'S RD., NORWICH

Telephone 1269

Correct
Golfing
Kit.

Plus-four Suits
Made to
Measure in Real
Harris Tweeds
...guineas.

...GOLF
...RS AND
...HOSE.

Hats and
...Best

...EENS TAILORS.

Telephone : 672

P. PROCTER

Pork Butcher and Purveyor
Ham and Bacon Curer

FRESH SAUSAGES DAILY
(Guaranteed all Pork)
...LTRY & GAME IN SEASON
...KED MEATS A SPECIALITY

...ls delivered to an...

35 St. Stephe...
NORWI...

The mark of
maximum length
and toughness

LOOK FOR THE IDENTIFICATION DOTS
SEE THE NAMES 'SPALDING' & 'TOP-FLITE'

SPA...

Needled TO...

...make no mistake about the name...

BERT KELLY

PROFESSIONAL GOLFER

All requisites for the game supplied. Largest
selected stock in the county.

CLUB, BAGS, SHOES, CLOTHING, ETC.

Tuition by Appointment.

EATON NORWICH GOLF CLUB
NORWICH

Telephone: NORWICH 52478

BOWHILL & ELLIOTT

FAMILY AND MILITARY
BOOT AND SHOE MAKERS

65 LONDON ST
NORWICH

REPAIRS

TELEPHONE :
116

Ask for
LAMBERT'S TEA
it's more economical

Whole...
Blend...

F. LAMBERT AND SON LTD... NORWICH, IPSWICH and GT. YARMOUTH

Advertisements from
The Eaton Golf Club
Official Handbook *over
the years.*

DANGER
BEWARE OF
FLYING
GOLF BALLS

green. The magnificent 8th was played from the current 7th tee to the present 8th green – just imagine the prospect of that drive over the woods. The 9th was from its existing tee to a green roughly placed where the putting green now is with Kelly's shop backing on to the boundary hedge. The 10th continued on its present course, past the tumulus to the edge of the slope down to the lower part of the course. Lastly the 11th was a blind drive from the top of the tumulus in Medal play, or from the edge of the bluff in general play, to the present green.

Over the subsequent decades all these holes have been altered because of the residential developments along our borders and it is generally recognised none for the better. This problem still confronts us today with some neighbours alongside the 11th being troubled by occasional badly sliced or shanked tee shots.

Mary Rust (Davies) 1964
'A golfing machine named Mary Rust won the Norfolk women's championship at Sheringham yesterday' EDP.

Opposite: View from 7th tee taken by Richard Tilbrook in 1985.

1960s

Once again this decade was one of relatively little change. However one significant local event which was to impact on Eaton Golf Club was the reduction of the municipal course at Earlham to nine holes in 1963 and its subsequent closure in 1965 to make way for the construction of the University of East Anglia. Many members of the popular Earlham club were to join Eaton and five day membership was introduced at this time in order to accommodate them. Once more the membership stood at a healthy 500 compared to the 350 of the immediate post war years, with a consequent improvement in the bank balance. This sudden influx of new members, both male and female, increased the pressure on clubhouse facilities which were little changed since the replacement building following the fire of 1921. Therefore the Dining Room and Ladies Lounge were added in 1965 with further major changes, such as the creation of a new entrance and extension to the Card Room, following shortly after.

Yet another Exhibition match was played in 1962 involving Dai Rees, Bernard Hunt,

Dave Thomas and now TV commentator Peter Allis. An amusing anecdote from the game involved the two Welsh pros Rees and Thomas: the latter was well known for his fiery temper and big hitting. On the 16th he badly hooked his second shot out of bounds over Marston Lane and proceeded to stomp off down the fairway in a rage. Rees called him back and reminded him that people had paid good money to watch him play golf and that he should put down another ball, which he duly did!

1970s

This was the decade in which most of the alterations to the 1948 course layout mentioned earlier took place and the design as we know it today was finally created.

The first changes were necessitated by the hazard to residential properties on the neighbouring Eaton Rise. The 6th hole abandoned the green in the furthest corner by the chalk pits and play was re-routed to the old 7th green. The present 7th green was constructed and a new 8th tee made adjacent to the 1st green. These new holes were open for play in late 1970.

The next holes to be lost/changed were the 10th, where a new green was created in front of the tumulus, thus shortening the hole by some 80 yards, and the abandonment of the 11th tee on top of the tumulus for a new tee below the bluff.

The final change was the shortening of the 9th from a rather innocuous par 4 to a good par 3, which made much needed space available near the clubhouse. This enabled the construction of a practice putting green, which had previously been by the flower beds in front of the clubhouse windows, a much improved trolley storage facility and, most importantly, vastly superior accommodation for the Professional and for greenstaff and their equipment.

All this meant that, save a few new hazards, by the end of the decade the course as we play it in our Centenary Year was finally settled upon.

In 1977 it was discovered that a small parcel of land, some 692 square yards between the 7th tee and green, was not owned by the Gurney Trust but by Norwich City Council from whom the club purchased it for £250. A small start was made towards our eventual acquisition of the entire site!

45

Bert Kelly being presented with his retirement gift by Captain Jock Munro. Also pictured left to right Phil Sheridan, Val Munro, Bill Palmer and Hubert Clay.

1980s

In 1972 the club had voted at an EGM for the installation of an automatic watering system (pop-up sprinklers). However the membership failed to agree on the financing. Some ten years later the sprinklers were up and running. Such are the machinations of most golf clubs I suspect!

The course has used its own water supply for many years. The pumphouse is located by the 11th green and it is fed by an underground spring which runs beneath the 11th and 4th greens.

The 'Men Only' stud bar was incorporated into the main Lounge area in 1989. This is where the TV now stands. Initially there was no television set and there was much deliberation at Committee over the years as to whether we should install one. This sounds very familiar since in July 1934 the House Committee decided 'not to install wireless apparatus in the clubhouse'.

Undoubtedly the most significant event of the 80s was the retirement, in June 1983, of Bert Kelly and his brother and assistant Fred, thus ending a tenure of 44 years, and a continuous relationship between the family and Eaton Golf Club spanning no fewer than 71 years.

A plan had been hatched in 1983 to regain some of the yardage lost in the previous decade. Norwich City Council had agreed to lease the club land on the south side of the 14th tee with a view to draining it and by using landfill from the construction of the southern bypass to build it up so a new hole, or even two, could be built. Plans were drawn up with the aid of a golf course architect and all seemed to be going smoothly. Sadly the venture floundered at the planning

View of marshland from 14th tee where we had hoped to extend the course

stage when local residents raised objections to the lorries which would bring the landfill, even though these were to be limited to two per day! Even the local MP and Lord Mayor became involved in discussions with Captain Dennis Lister. There was also some discussion about putting the 12th tee back to its original position (i.e. in the marsh level with the 16th green with access via a causeway) – this also did not come to fruition.

Drawing of Clubhouse in 2006 by Ken Taylor (Yorkshire & England Cricket, Huddersfield Town FC and Slade School of Art).

1990s It's ours!

Almost since the inception of the club many attempts had been made to persuade the Gurney Trustees to sell us the freehold of the golf course. Royal Norwich had been successful in a purchase bid in 1894 from the same landlords.

The terms of the first lease were negotiated by 'Jack' Read way back in 1910. As reported to the inaugural meeting on 20th September of that year an annual rent of £30 would be payable for a term of seven years on the 40 acres now representing the upper section of the course. Concerns were expressed that the short-term lease would be a stumbling block but 'Jack' Read reassured those present that a renewal was almost certain in due course.

With the desire to extend the course to 18 holes the remaining land on the city side of Marston Lane was leased from JH Gurney in 1912.

The lease to rent the land between the present 10th hole and Newmarket Road, some 30 acres, was set up in 1923. This area is now the top end of Greenways and what was the Civil Service Sports Ground. Three years later the club sought an extension to the lease in order to secure its future. John Gurney expressed the thought that

The presence of the golf course would enhance the possibility of housing development and that once approval had been granted for planning proposals a long lease would be granted.

Although such dwellings took many years to appear on our boundaries, the lease was extended.

The final extension of the leased land came in 1931 when the land to the south of Marston Lane (31 acres) was acquired on a 20 year lease at an annual rent of £143 10s plus Land Tax, Property Tax and Tithe. This followed an apparently unsuccessful bid in 1930 to purchase the freehold from the Gurney Trust. One condition of the new lease was that the land rented in 1923 should be surrendered as it duly was in 1935.

Over the years the lease was regularly renewed and the rent increased. However, in 1990 the Gurney Trustees made it clear that they were unlikely to renew the lease when it expired in 2002. Since 1985 the role of Chairman of Forward Planning had existed and Jack Abel had been given the brief of finding out the views of the Trustees and of investigating the options available to the club. At this stage the Trustees were, perhaps understandably, unprepared to commit themselves as to their position 17 years hence.

49

Therefore on 24th March 1990 a first meeting of interested members was held regarding the surrender of the lease and the future, if one existed, of Eaton Golf Club. At this time the club was totally reliant on the Gurney Trustees agreeing to help the Club relocate to an alternative venue.

Indeed the Club's position was perilous; the top section of the course, site of the original nine holes, appeared to be prime land for development and, dependant on planning permission being granted that seemed to be the intention of the Gurney Trustees. We seemed to be in an impossible situation. So it was in 1993 Colin Brown, our Centenary Captain, was asked by the Committee of Management to become Chairman of Forward Planning in order to develop a strategy to take the Club beyond 2002.

Colin had joined the Club two years earlier and had been on the Management Committee since 1992. He was a solicitor specialising in Property law. His initial observation was:

Why should the Trustees help provide an alternative golf course for the Club when they could have the land for nothing in 2002?

In October 1993 a tentative offer to see how keen the Trustees were to sell was rejected, principally because the owners were concerned about losing the development potential of the site, which would inevitably increase its value several fold. However, sufficient interest had been shown to suggest that, if a proposal could be found that allowed the Trustees to share in any subsequent development of the site for any purpose other than its current use as a golf course, they might be prepared to enter into negotiations.

The lack of a 'plan' was becoming a problem; some members were seeking alternative sites to secure their future golf in the uncertainty of Eaton's destiny. Therefore it was agreed to draw up a small team led by Colin Brown who would work to prepare a feasibility study of moving Eaton Golf Club to an alternative location. On 12th August 1993 an EGM was held at the CNS to explain the current situation to members. The members present, nearly 300, voted by an overwhelming majority to pursue negotiations with the landlords for a financial package to relocate EGC. The only bargaining weapon at our disposal was to agree to an early surrender of the remaining years on the lease with the Gurney Trust in return for help

21st May 1997:
The Directors of Eaton
Golf Club (Norwich)
Limited look on as the
legal documents which
secure the freehold are
signed.

Back row: Mark
Hardwick (Competition),
Roger Burton
(Membership),
Alan Nichols (Captain),
Elizabeth Clayton
(Lady Captain),
Michael Hull (Green),
Richard Harvey (House).

Front row: Dennis Lister
(Finance), David
Chapman (Chairman),
Colin Brown (Forward
Planning).

with relocating the Club to another venue. The initial proposal was to develop a course on land at Bramerton. Draft plans had been drawn up to include 27 holes, a clubhouse and driving range.

However there was no way the Club could finance such a venture – it was estimated that close to £1m would be needed. This required the Gurney Trust to buy the land and donate it to the Club

who would, in turn, have to fund the development of a course. However the Gurneys did not have the money to purchase and were reliant on a nominated developer of the land at Eaton to come up with the money. In the meantime agents for the owner of the Bramerton site had decided to put the site up for sale to 'best offers' and indeed the Gurney Trust was out-bid. Thus the option of a move to Bramerton seemed to have disappeared.

In June 1995 all thoughts were being directed to the purchase of Weston Park as an alternative site from the then owner Roy Benton. Yet again this was not to prove easy. Mr Benton's health was failing and he was keen to sell quickly, but had been advised to sell the golf course and the adjoining Dinosaur Park as a complete package, therefore raising the price way above the amount potentially available to Eaton. With his death at the end of that month it became clear that his executors were only prepared to go for a 'best price' offer, therefore effectively putting Eaton and the Gurneys out of the market.

With Bramerton and Weston Park gone, the only viable option was to focus all our efforts on a plan to stay at Eaton. As we entered 1996 a new Captain, Mike Fenn was installed; he too was an ardent supporter of the 'stand and fight' campaign. Moreover a new role had been created within the Club structure, that of Chairman of the Committee of Management; David Chapman was appointed as the first incumbent in May. Along with Dennis Lister as Treasurer and Colin Brown this trio were to be the driving force behind the moves to purchase Eaton. In a letter to the members in early 1996 Colin Brown had set out to the membership the strengths of the club in relation to the Gurney Trustees:

- the fighting fund, which now stood at £370k
- the strong resolve of a membership of 800
- a settled intention to stay at Eaton
- six years in which to formulate plans – namely the period before the lease was to expire in 2002.
- the public support which could be generated for an anti-development campaign.

There were several issues that stood in the way of the Gurneys obtaining planning permission for residential development of the land. Firstly the land on the lower part of the course was 'green belt' but it was thought that they might offer this to the Council to maintain as a 'pay-and-play' golf

facility as a 'sweetener'. The land above the valley also had many restrictions, such as the ancient burial mounds and many of the established wooded areas that would have to be preserved; there were problems of access and the council's policy on the provision of low-cost housing. All of these factors were likely to drive down the price of the land, thus enabling the Club to make a realistic bid.

The future of the land was fast becoming a burning issue in the locality; several articles had appeared in the local press and it was clear that any development of Eaton Golf Club was going to be a controversial affair. The Gurneys had caught wind of this, and in April 1996 the Club received a letter from the Trustees which read:

> *Some time ago we discussed the possibility of the Club buying all or some of the course ... .*
> *Is this possibility alive or dead?*

This was the first real indication that there was a willingness to sell to the Club. It was now a question of 'how much' rather than 'if'. The figures ranged from £2m, which the Club's advisors thought the Trustees would be likely to ask and £1.2m, which the Club thought it could afford. Eventually the Forward Planning Committee decided to make an offer of £1.75m.

One condition of a sale was that the Gurneys would retain a parcel of land, most of the 10th fairway for future development, which would necessitate the re-design of the 10th and 18th holes. However they were prepared to offer a 10 year lease on this land rent-free.

On 18th February 1997 a formal offer of £1.75m was made to the Gurney Trustees. If accepted this would trigger an EGM to seek the approval of the membership. On 5th March the offer was accepted, so an EGM was set for 9th April at the UEA. Chairman David Chapman had

written to the members outlining how the purchase would be funded. A fixed-interest mortgage of £850k had been arranged which, with £390k from the Development Fund, would finance the bulk of the purchase. In excess of £280k had been pledged by members as either gifts or interest free loans. It was proposed that the residue should be raised by the issue of Loan Bonds of £400; payable by all members, except Junior, Intermediate, Honorary Life and Non-playing categories. This would be redeemable either on death or cessation of membership and a new member joining.

The Committee was naturally delighted, and somewhat relieved, when the membership endorsed their proposed purchase plan at the ensuing EGM. So it was on 27th May 1997 the purchase of the golf course by the newly formed Eaton Golf Club (Norwich) Ltd was completed.

An enormous debt of gratitude was due to the main participants in this historic phase in the Club's history and in particular to Colin Brown, David Chapman and Dennis Lister who had worked so hard to secure the future of Eaton Golf Club for generations of golfers to come.

2005 'The Last Piece of the Jigsaw'

In January 2004 Colin Brown, who had stepped down from the Committee in 1998 following the purchase of the course, approached then Chairman Ron McDonald to suggest that he should re-engage the Gurney Trustees and begin negotiating the purchase of the 10th hole. After some months of discussion a figure of £225k emerged as the 'right price'. It appeared to be a good deal and it gave the Club the opportunity to review its borrowing facilities. The £225k would be added to the outstanding loan and a new mortgage set up over a 20 year period, thus making the purchase virtually cost neutral to existing members. On 15th January 2005 an EGM was called at the CNS. After a presentation by Colin Brown those present voted unanimously in favour of the deal and the purchase was completed some weeks later.

Thus the entire site was now owned by the Club, effectively the membership. In summary, Colin said in his recollection of these monumental events:

The 13 years of discussion, negotiation, arguing, letter writing, cajoling and persuasion had been worthwhile. We owned the freehold of our golf course and that was what the members had always hoped for.

The Professionals

In which we serve

Over the century of its existence Eaton Golf Club has been very fortunate to be served by many loyal, talented and enthusiastic individuals. The members, who have given freely of their time to serve on various committees, the professionals, greenstaff, clubhouse staff and secretaries have all contributed to the development of the very special place that is Eaton Golf Club.

W Sutton 1910–12

The club's first Professional of whom little is known except that he was clearly a fine golfer. The EDP reported that on 18th August 1911 whilst playing with member W Bradley, *Sutton went out in 34 and came back in 34 – total 68. This is 12 below bogey.*

'Dick' Kelly, driving, watched by Ernest Riseborough, left, George Pilch plus AN Other.

R (Dick) Kelly 1912–46

Dick Kelly moved to Norfolk from his home in North Berwick (Scotland) in 1893 to take up the post of Professional at the newly formed Royal Norwich Golf Club. He had previously worked for Ben Sayers, the pro at Berwick and renowned club maker. During his spell at the club he took part in several 'exhibition' matches – similar to those staged at Eaton in later years – which were designed to create interest in the game locally. Most particularly, in 1895, he played against reigning Open Champion JH Taylor who was to be called upon to lay out the first 18 hole course at Eaton.

He was also matched against James Braid, another Open Champion, one year later and as the Royal Norwich archives record: 'the local professional held his own respectably against this high-class opposition on most occasions'.

In 1901 he moved to Mundesley. Whilst there he met up with the third member of the 'Great Triumverate', Harry Vardon, who was recuperating from TB at the nearby Kelling Sanatorium. Vardon, Braid and Taylor were recognised as the founders of the 'modern' game of golf, so Kelly clearly moved in lofty circles and was apparently held in high esteem by his fellow pros.

In 1910 his move to Eaton began a family link with our club the like of which few others can boast. Not only was he a fine player but apparently a well-respected teacher of the game – so important in a club where many members were new to the game. Indeed the Kelly family was responsible for hundreds of Norwich families learning how to play the game. Their hallmark was a 'natural' approach, whereby players, having learned the rudimentary skills, were encouraged to develop their game within their own limitations rather than try to swing it like Vardon & Co.

Dick had eight children, four of whom followed him into the golf profession. George was the Professional at Royal Norwich for many years, Russell was the pro at Morley, near Wymondham, which like Eaton was cultivated during the war but was never restarted afterwards, so he moved to a driving range near London whilst Bert and Fred carried on the family tradition at Eaton.

Bert Kelly 1939–83 and Fred Kelly 1946–83

Bert, the youngest of the Kelly boys, joined his father as joint Professional in August 1939. However, fairly soon after taking up the post war broke out and Bert joined the Royal Artillery. He spent most of the war years as a POW of the Germans in camps in Eastern Europe. As the Russians advanced in winter 1944 he was force-marched, along with thousands of fellow allied prisoners, over 750 miles as the Wehrmacht troops retreated. He suffered severe frostbite in the process but always considered himself fortunate as many of his comrades failed to make it. After liberation he spent four months at Sunningdale trying to regain his enthusiasm for the game of golf.

Bert Kelly left, with brothers Fred and George.

In 1938 Bert had not only won his first Norfolk professional title but also had played in his first Open Championship at Royal St George's. During his playing career he went on to win three further County titles, the East Anglian Open twice and to play in four more Opens. Widely recognised as a supreme striker of the ball Bert, by his own admission, was at best a 'streaky' putter. This no doubt held him back from reaching the very top flight of playing professionals.

He took sole charge in 1946 and appointed his brother, Fred, who had been working in the shoe trade, as his assistant. As a club pro Bert was very much one of the 'old school'. The brothers were skilled and patient teachers and Bert was often out playing nine with the members. They served the Club and its members with charm and dignity, and both always seemed to have time to chat or pass on a few anecdotes or playing tips. As a youngster I would spend many a summer's afternoon with Fred in his workshop or making him a pot of tea to share on the seat outside the shop where he would puff gently on his ever present pipe (Players Whisky Flake) and chat idly about this and that. He called me 'boy' and often let me 'help' in the workshop – I learned to whip clubs and was a dab hand at winding on leather grips (at least Fred was too gentle to tell me otherwise!).

On his retirement, in 1983, Bert was made an Honorary Life Member although he rarely played thereafter. He calculated that the family had served Eaton for a combined total of 140 years.

Frank Hill 1983–95

Frank started his professional golfing career at Sherwood Forest Golf Club and moved to Selsdon Park Golf Club in 1965, the first year he played in the Open Championship at Royal Birkdale. In 1977 he moved to Norfolk as pro at Great Yarmouth and Caister Golf Club from where he won the East Anglian Championship. During his tenure at Eaton Frank's son James came to prominence; firstly as a Junior then in the full County side for whom he never lost a singles match. James won the Norfolk Open at Sheringham as an amateur after which he turned Pro.

Frank is a prodigious striker of a golf ball and has enjoyed considerable success on the Seniors Tour, including several top ten finishes on the European Seniors' Tour. In 2006 he won the prestigious PGA National Super Seniors' Championship.

Most importantly, Frank continued the tradition of Club Professionals at Eaton – one of gentle dignity and charm combined with fine playing and teaching skills. He is currently Senior Pro at Thorpeness Golf Club on the Suffolk coast.

Above: Frank Hill playing in the Turkish Seniors Open.

Top: James Hill holding the Norfolk Open Trophy.

61

Robert Foster

Robert was Assistant to Frank Hill and went on to be Pro at Great Yarmouth. He won the Norfolk Open playing out of Eaton. He also played for two years on the European Tour.

Mark Spooner

Mark was also one of Frank's Assistants. He too won the Norfolk Open. He has gone on to be a teaching pro at Bawburgh Golf Club.

Dean Futter and Nigel Bundy

Dean Futter and Nigel Bundy also had brief spells as Professional following Frank Hill.

Mark Allen 1997–

Mark joined our club from Thetford where he had played as a Junior and had served as Assistant to Norman Arthur. He is a well-respected player on the local circuit, and in 2001 shot a remarkable 61 at Eaton in an NPGA Pro-Am, a record low score for the NPGA (admittedly off the winter tees). He has three times reached the final qualifying stages for The Open and has played three times in the Club Professionals' Championship. His fellow pros have twice elected him to serve as Captain of the NPGA and in 2007 he won their Matchplay Championship. In 2008 he accompanied three club members to an NPGA Pro-Am in Northern France where he won the Professional prize and the team also triumphed.

The Players

Over the years many Eaton golfers have distinguished themselves both at club and county level. With apologies to the many fine players whom I do not mention in the lines below, here follows a brief 'biography' of the more notable.

FV (Fred) Spalding

One of the earliest members of the Club of whom little is known except that on 29th June 1920 he received a letter from the then Secretary informing him of his scratch handicap – the first to achieve that honour. He was elected an Honorary Life Member in 1931.

Morris Scratch Cup 1923 and 1924

Hines Cup 1925 and 1926

ST (Sidney) Gill

If any one person merits the sobriquet 'Mr Eaton Club' it is Sidney Gill. We have already read of his generous gesture of building the new clubhouse at cost, to a Stanley Wearing plan, following the devastating fire of 1921, and of his designs for the extended 18 hole course to incorporate the 'over the road' holes in 1931. Indeed it is worth noting again that the course we play today is in essence pure 'Sidney'. He was also a scratch golfer in his prime and continued playing into his late eighties; he managed to extend his playing career by purchasing a vivid blue golf cart in the 1960s. He was Captain 1925–26 and President for a remarkable

ST (Sidney) Gill

seventeen years from 1943 to 1960. In 1954 he was awarded the MBE for services to the building industry. He was an Honorary Life Member.

R G Pilch

Captain 1928. Founder of the family Sports Shop in Brigg Street in 1903. Not only a County golfer but he also played cricket, hockey and soccer for Norfolk for many years.

Hines Cup 1927

Morris Scratch Cup 1923 and 1928

Norfolk County Team

George Pilch

Son of RG Pilch, brother of Myra and father of David – all county players – George was the mainstay of the County team for over a decade. He also played hockey and squash for Norfolk. As a member of Norfolk's premier sporting family George was invited to play in many memorable exhibition matches. Apart from that against Max Faulkner and Charlie Ward in 1950 he also played against the legendary American, Walter Hagen, at Royal Norwich where the family have strong links and another Open Champion, Bobby Locke at Caister. Contemporary newspaper reports suggest that the young George more than held his own in such illustrious company.

George Pilch, in plus fours, playing the legendary American, Walter Hagen at Royal Norwich.

Ward Cup 1928–29

Morris Scratch Cup 1946

Hines Cup 1930, 1949 and 1956

Quite an achievement to win the record low gross score of the year in three decades.

Norfolk County Team

Norfolk County Captain 1952–55

Geoffrey Burroughes

He won more scratch events in his era than any other player. The County Handicap trophy is The Geoffrey Burroughes Salver. He was also a member of Royal Norwich – it appears that many golfers at that time were members of more than one club.

Morris Scratch Cup 1936, 1939 and 1947

Hines Cup 1926, 1932, 1936 and 1937

The pinnacle of his golfing career was winning the Norfolk Amateur Championship in 1937 – the first from Eaton to do so.

John Clymer

After playing all his early golf at Eaton, John went on to be a prominent member at Royal Norwich and Great Yarmouth and Caister golf clubs, where he dominated the honours boards for many years – as any visitor can see.

He was one of the few Eaton golfers to receive international honours.

Ward Junior Cup 1930, 1932, 1933 and 1934

Morris Scratch Cup 1937–38

Hines Cup 1939 and 1946

England Boys International 1935 and 1936

Norfolk Amateur Champion 1947

Norfolk Open Champion 1950

Norfolk County Team

Sid Cranmer

Sid was a junior member at Dereham. Whilst he continued to play there over the years, and was the course record holder, it was at Eaton that he rose to prominence not only at club but also very much at County level. His dominance of club scratch competitions speaks for itself and is never likely to be equalled. He was powerfully built and a long hitter in his prime, but he was an exquisite chipper and putter even into his golfing autumn. It was a quirk of fate that his 'glory' years coincided with those of the great Arthur Perowne. Perowne was a Walker Cup player and, but for him, Sid surely would have won many more County Championships.

(I had the good fortune to play occasional golf with Sid in later years and recall him recording nine consecutive threes from the 6th to the 14th in a 'friendly' fourball!)

Morris Scratch Cup 9 times between 1949 and 1972

Hines Cup 12 times between 1948 and 1979

Norfolk Amateur Champion 1971 and 1972
(Runner-up 3 times)

Norfolk Seniors Champion 1982 and 1985

Norfolk County Team

Ivor Dunnell

Whilst Sid dominated the scratch competitions in his era no other golfer has come near Ivor's record of success over the years (nor is anyone likely to). He was a member of Earlham and when it closed in 1963 he moved to Royal Norwich, like so many others. After three years he joined Eaton. He has won 34 Major trophies during his time at the Club. Never the longest hitter, Ivor was Mr Consistency and a doughty competitor. Moreover he has probably played more rounds at Eaton than any other golfer since he used to work night shifts at Eastern Counties Newspapers leaving his days free for his beloved golf. He also represented the county at bowls.

For 13 years he ran the Junior Section in tandem with Nan Holloway, and was instrumental in encouraging many of today's prominent players in their formative years.

Golf apart, Ivor was also a very talented pianist who toured Europe with a professional band just after the war; who can forget his impromptu performances at Club Christmas parties?

However the pinnacle of his career must have been qualifying for the English Amateur in 1972 at Royal St George's where he narrowly lost 2 & 1 to five times winner Michael Bonnallack.

Norfolk County Team

Norfolk County Foursomes

Club Trophies; too many to list but he has won the Hines Cup,

Morris Scratch Cup

Varnon Cup

Victory Cup

Sidney Gill Cup

Captains Prize

Stanley Wearing Foursomes

Arthur Lock Bowl

and George Green Cup

Several of these were multiple wins.

Peter Johnston

Peter was Captain of Golf at Cambridge University before moving to Norwich.

Although he left the Club at a relatively early age, those who saw him play say that he was the most technically correct and complete golfer to play at Eaton.

Hines Cup 1971 (68 gross – Amateur Course Record)

Norfolk County Amateur Champion 1970

Norfolk County Team – in his four years in the side he never lost a singles match.

Left to right: Peter Johnson, Sid Cranmer and Ivor Dunnell, winners of County Scratch Team Shield in 1971 being presented with the trophy by John Quinton (President) and Frank Nicholls (Captain).

Mike Orr

Mike played golf at Eaton as a junior in the 1960s. His victory in the Amateur was in horrendous weather at Hunstanton. Apparently, whilst everybody else was swathed in bulky waterproof clothing, Mike stripped to his shirtsleeves, got soaked and kept battling away to an unexpected but thoroughly deserved win. He was an Oxford golf 'blue' for three years.

Norfolk Amateur Champion 1973

County Team Events

The club carried off the Scratch Team Shield in 1938, 1939, 1947, 1955, 1967, 1968 and 1971.

The Juniors have also won their equivalent trophy in 1980, 1981, 1983, 1984, 1988 and 1993.

Club Championship

With the advent of The Club Championship in 1981 we had for the first time a tangible measure of the 'best' golfer of the year. The following are those who have won that honour on at least three occasions.

'The Mammoth Niblick', the Club Champions Trophy.

Brian Walker

An elegant player who took to golf relatively late in life, Brian was, and remains, a sublime putter. He has that extraordinary ability to, in his own words, 'change gear' in mid round and make a birdie just when needed.

In times of sudden cloudbursts we should all be grateful to Brian, as he gave the club the various shelters dotted around the course – sheet roofing is his business. Also, in 2004 he kindly donated The Walker Cup, a trophy played for by Seniors (55+) off scratch and a smaller handicap cup.

Hines Cup 1967, 1978 and 1981

Morris Scratch Cup 1970, 1976, 1978 and 1988

Club Champion 1983, 1084, 1991 and 1992

Norfolk Seniors Champion 1990 and 1991

Austin Brydon

Without question the most dedicated golfer I've seen. From a very early age Austin was to be seen hitting endless practice balls or on the putting green fine-tuning his short game. It clearly paid off, as his record of achievement is unparalleled in the modern era. Austin moved to Royal Norwich in 2000, where he thought he might find

stiffer competition and a more challenging course. He played most of his early golf at Eaton and we are very proud of him.

Hines Cup 1988, 1994 and 1998

Morris Scratch Cup 1993, 1997,1998 and 1999

Club Champion 1986, 1987, 1988 and 1997 (His 36 hole total of 136 – two under standard scratch – in 1988 remains the lowest recorded.)

Norfolk Junior Champion 1985

Norfolk Amateur Champion 2003 and 2007

Norfolk County Foursomes (twice with ex-Eaton member Chris Lamb)

Norfolk Open Champion 1990

Norfolk County Team

Norfolk County Captain 1995–97

He has also played in the English & British Matchplay Championships and the Brabazon Trophy (English Strokeplay)

Marcus Barrett

Marcus' talent for the game was evident from an early age. He appears very 'laid-back', almost casual, when playing, but beneath there hides a steely resolve. Few amateurs have won the Norfolk Open, in so doing beating all the Club Professionals; Marcus was the youngest, aged just 17. Moreover he successfully defended the title the following year. Marcus hit the junior heights when he won the East Region Daily Mail Tournament thus qualifying for the National Finals held at Lake Nona in Florida, USA. There he was runner-up, by a solitary stroke, to Graeme Storm, now a top-flight tour pro, and beating Paul Casey and Luke Donald in the process. He also gained International honours by being selected for the England Youth squad in 1996.

Hines Cup 1995, 2000 and 2001

Morris Scratch Cup 2000

Club Champion 1994, 1996 and 2002

Norfolk Open Champion 1995 and 1996

Norfolk County Team

John Maddock

A PE teacher at Earlham High School, John came to Eaton from Gorleston. He continues to play his County golf in Suffolk.

Club Champion 1989, 1990, 1993 and 1995

Suffolk Amateur Champion

Suffolk Open Champion

Suffolk County Team

Prince of Wales Cup (played at Royal St George's)

Alan and Andrew Nicholls

Alan, father of Andrew was the first winner of the Club Championships in 1981. He also won the prestigious

Andrew and Alan Nicholls

Moray Open, one of the premier Scottish Amateur competitions. Andrew followed his father and won our Club Championship in 2006, thus being the only father and son to win the 'big one'.

Andrew is also the current holder of the Amateurs Course Record with a gross 64.

EATON GOLF CLUB												

COMPETITION VARNON CUP
DATE 5.8.90 TIME
PLAYER A A.K. NICHOLS Handicap 5
PLAYER B

Hole	Markers Score	Summer Yards	Par	Winter Yards	Stroke Index	GROSS SCORE A	B	W + H = O Points	NETT SCORE	Ladies Yards	Par	Stroke Index
1		478	5	452	17	5				439	5	7
2		159	3	138	9	3				102	3	17
3		457	4	420	1	4				419	5	13
4		417	4	385	3	3				362	4	3
5		518	5	496	11	5				481	5	1
6		355	4	335	5	4				319	4	5
7		190	3	164	7	2				179	3	11
8		348	4	332	15	4				340	4	9
9		194	3	170	13	3				151	3	15
OUT		3116	35	2892		33				2792	36	OUT

PLEASE AVOID SLOW PLAY AT ALL TIMES

10		361	4	341	6	4				348	4	6
11		163	3	152	16	2				152	3	16
12		352	4	335	2	3				327	4	2
13		161	3	134	18	3				135	3	18
14		350	4	333	14	3				316	4	10
15		336	4	328	10	4				305	4	14
16		510	5	487	8	5				469	5	4
17		301	4	289	12	3				274	4	12
18		468	4	434	4	4				444	5	8
IN		3002	35	2833		31				2770	36	IN
OUT		3116	35	2892		33				2792	36	OUT
TOTAL		6118	70	5725		64				5562	72	TOTAL

Holes won 5
Holes lost 59
Result

Men's Amateur Course Record

David Wilson

Scratch golfer David gained his first international honours when selected to play for England Under 14s in 1998 and 1999. He has played Norfolk County golf at all levels from Under 14 to first team. In 2001 he finished tied 1st in the English Under 16 Schools Championships and was subsequently selected to play for England against Wales. He has won our Club Championship in 2005/07/08 and the prestigious Caister Candelabra in 2005. In 2006 he also won the Norfolk Matchplay at Sheringham. After a spell working with Mark Allen in the Pro Shop David has decided to pursue a career in golf at Birmingham University. In his first year he was unbeaten in 14 inter-university league singles matches and has helped his team qualify for the World Student Championships in Germany.

David Wilson
ADRIAN JUDD, EASTERN DAILY PRESS

The Ladies

Miss M Long

Clearly a very able player since Margaret was a Junior England International in 1938. She won the Hines Cup for Girls in 1936/7 as did her sister the following year. Her parents also played at Eaton. She played County golf for Norfolk. After marrying she moved to Woking where she played for Surrey for many years.

Margaret Long (girl with striped tie behind lady holding trophy) England v Scotland 1938 at Stoke Poges GC.

M Martin (née Pilch)

No family has been more synonymous with Norfolk golf than the Pilch dynasty. Myra, like her brother George, played County golf through three decades. She was Eaton Ladies' Captain in 1933 and again as Mrs Martin in 1949. She was County Champion in 1950 and Captain in 1953.

J Brister (née Cowell)

Playing out of Earlham as Miss Cowell she won the County Championship in 1951 and 1957. She also went on to win the Veterans' County title. She also played County golf for many years, captaining the side in 1961/2 and again in 1974/5. She was elected County President from 1988–91. She presented the Brister Salver to NCLGA to be played for by

Mary Davies (née Rust)

No Eaton golfer, male or female, has dominated Norfolk County golf more than Mary. Although she was also a member of Royal Cromer – the Rusts had a chain of grocers' stores throughout North Norfolk – she won eight County Ladies' Championships between 1962 and 1987 playing out of Eaton.

She was County Vets' Champion four times.

She Captained both the County 1st team, twice, and the Veterans'.

In 1993, 1995 and 2000 she won the Eaton Ladies' Championship, leaving many players up to 40 years her junior trailing in her wake.

those who had played County 2nd team golf in that year. Jenny Tyler won it in 1993.

Lady Captain 1980 and President 1995–6.

Above: Mary Davies.

Left: Jill Brister on her way to winning the County Championshop in 1951.

Grace Rampling (née Bousfield)

It would not be out of order to label Grace as 'Mrs Eaton Golf Club'. This is not necessarily in recognition of her play, but for her tireless devotion to her beloved Eaton. She joined the Club in 1920 and was still playing a regular nine holes into her nineties some 71 years later! Indeed she had the same locker, No 7, throughout all that time. She was Lady Captain in 1946/7 as Miss Bousfield and again in 1953. In 1970/72 she was Lady President. She was elected an Honorary Life Member in 1982. She also devoted herself to County golf – she held the Presidency from 1984-7 and served as Treasurer for no less than 38 years.

In recognition of the pleasure Eaton had brought her she presented the Ladies section with a silver cigarette box in 1948, to be played for by 'business ladies', a crystal bowl awarded to the lady with the lowest nett score on Lady President's Day, and in 1971 the Lady President's chain of office.

'Mrs Eaton Golf Club', Grace Rampling, member for over 70 years pictured with Frank Nicholls (left) and 'Big Fred' Freddie Francis all of whom played golf into their late 80s.

Lyndsey (Harris) Hewison

Lady Captain 1990. Lyndsey was unbeatable at the turn of the millennium. She was Club Champion in 2001, 2002 and 2003 and played for the County 1st team.

At the height of her powers Lyndsey set a Course Record of 70, two below Standard Scratch. She is also one of the Lady winners of the Arthur Lock mixed knockout. Lyndsey is well known and respected in local golfing circles in her role as golf correspondent for Eastern Counties Newspapers. She was Lady Captain in 1990. She has also been honoured by being appointed press officer for the English Women's Golf Association.

Melanie Chapmen

Melanie is the daughter of eminent members David and Sue Chapman. She won the Norfolk Girls Championship in 1987 and 1988.

With Lyndsey Hewison she won the Carrick Cup – a county foursomes scratch knockout – in 1988.

Partnered by mother Sue she won the County Foursomes in 1985.

She also played County 1st team golf for two years.

Karen Young

For a decade Karen shared the spoils at Eaton with Lyndsey. She won the Club Championship five times between 1994 and 2004 – a remarkable effort.

Even more noteworthy she has gone on to win the County Championship on an unprecedented three consecutive occasions; 2005, 2006 and 2007.

She also spread her wings and won the East Anglian title in 2004. Via this tournament she twice qualified for the English Ladies Championships.

She has been a prominent figure in the County team for several years and was Captain from 2002 till 2004.

It says much about Karen that she is one of a very few ladies who have won the Arthur Lock Rose Bowl, the mixed singles knockout at Eaton.

Edwina Lowry-Gold

Born in Australia, Edwina started playing golf at the age of 12. She moved to Norwich with her family a couple of years later, joined Eaton and swiftly made a mark on the golf scene at club, county and national levels. In 2005 she won our Ladies' Club Championship and the East Anglian Championship. A year later she won the Picken Trophy for the most improved Junior golfer in the East Region (the first girl to do so). She was also selected for the Norfolk Ladies team and was a semi-finalist in the Scottish Girls' which earned a call-up for the Scottish under 21 squad. In 2007 Edwina played for Scotland under 21s and reached the quarter-finals of the Scottish Amateur. She has had a remarkable five holes in one and holds three course

records including that of Eaton (see above). Playing off a handicap of 1 in 2008 Edwina won a prestigious golfing Scholarship to university in the States where her career will no doubt flourish.

Ladies' Amateur Course Record

Edwina Lowry-Gold right with Emma Davies

Emma Davies

Emma represents the next generation of fine Lady golfers from Eaton – she has also played hockey and badminton for the county at Junior level. Between 2006 and 2008 the list of her achievements is impressive; she has twice been Norfolk Under 18 Schools Champion (aged 15/16), twice won the Scratch County Foursomes with Edwina Lowrey-Gold, played County 2nd and 1st team, she was 3rd in the English Under 16 Championships and has played for Wales at Under 16 and Under 18 levels, culminating in 2008 with selection for the Welsh Under 16 Nations Cup team.

24 July 2009 – Emma Davies wins Welsh Under 18 Girls Championship at 20th hole and earns selection for Home Internationals.

77

Trophies

Most of the trophies, both men's and ladies', have been kindly donated over the years by members and, as such, provide a permanent reminder of their affection for the club. The following is a list of those trophies played for annually with the date they were first contested and a description of the nature of competition for which they are awarded.

Gentlemen's Trophies

Men's Trophies

George Green Cup (1911)

Presented by Alderman Green who appears not to have been a member.

Singles knockout.

Victory Cup (1919)

First staged to celebrate the end of The Great War.

18 hole stroke play.

Captain's Day Trophy (1920)

18 hole stroke play.

Colman Bowl (1921)

Presented by past Captain, President, from 1920 to 1932, and Lord Mayor JH Colman.

36 holes stroke play played over two days.

Hines Cup (1923)

Presented by EE Hines – Captain 1920–22 and President 1933–42.

18 hole scratch stroke play.

Morris Scratch Cup (1923)

Presented by FW Morris in his year of captaincy.

Lowest gross score recorded over the year's stroke play competitions.

Varnon Cup (1926)

Presented by Eric Varnon.

18 hole stroke play.

Leith Tankards (1926)

Presented by member Montagu Leith when he left the club to move to West Africa.

18 hole fourball better ball stroke play played over the four days of

the Easter weekend. Players may play on all four days but with a different partner each day.

Mason Bowl (1929)

Presented by Mrs CB Hill in memory of her father PH Mason.

18 hole stroke play veterans (over 60 years).

Liberator Salver (1945)

Presented by Lt Col Michael Phipps of 95th Combat Bomb Wing USAF who played the course while stationed in Norfolk during WWII.
It is named after the Liberator bomber that he flew.

18 hole stroke play.

Sidney Gill Cup (1956)

Presented by Sidney Gill Captain 1925–6 and President 1943–60.

18 hole stroke play qualifying round; top 16 go through to stroke play knockout.

Stanley Wearing Bowl (1957)

Presented by Stanley Wearing – Captain 1924, Hon Secretary and clubhouse designer.

Foursomes knockout.

Whitbread Trophy (1966)

Originally a mixed foursomes cup from the Earlham Golf Club and donated to the Club on its closure.

Now awarded for the lowest net aggregate of four rounds from the Sidney Gill Qualifying, Colman Bowl, Liberator Salver, Victory and Varnon Cups (i.e. for the most

consistent player in the 'major' stroke play competitions off handicap).

Clifford White Salver (1967)

18 hole stroke play for handicaps 18–28.

Presented by his family.

Friendship Cup (1975)

Presented by the James and Coldwell families, Captains in 1940 & 1941 respectively.

A fourball better ball stableford.

Thomas Clay Trophies (1976)

Presented by Hubert Clay in memory of his father Tom Clay past Captain, Treasurer, temporary Secretary and President. In total 25 years service.

A fourball better ball knock-out played off the winter tees.

Queen Elizabeth II Silver Jubilee Cup (1977)

Presented by Mr & Mrs Jack Spencer both past Presidents to mark 25 years on the throne.

A foursomes stableford played in any combination; ladies', men's or mixed.

Club Championship (1981)

Presented by that year's Captain Phil Sheridan.

18 hole scratch stroke play on Saturday with top 16 qualifying for second 18 holes on Sunday. The Champion golfer for that year is the one with the lowest 36 hole aggregate.

To mark its introduction Bert Kelly donated a 'Mammoth Niblick' as a trophy, which has pride of place above the bar.

Joe O'Donaghue Trophy (1983)

An interesting sculpture of a golfer presented by member Joe O'Donaghue.

Awarded to the golfer with the lowest aggregate total from any four monthly medals over the year.

Neville Parish Foursomes (1985)

Presented by member Neville Parish.

18 hole foursomes stableford from which top four pairs contest matchplay semi-finals and final.

James Phillips 75+ Cup (1988)

Presented by retiring President Jimmy Phillips who also devised the interesting format. Open to members whose combined age and handicap total 75 or more.

18 hole medal played on any weekday in a given week in September. Coincidentally, Jimmy won it in its first year!

Club Championship (Handicap) Salver (1989)

Presented by past Captain Ted Vallis.

36 holes stroke play under handicap played on the same basis as the Scratch Championship.

Budge Foster Salver (1990)

Presented by Walter 'Budge' Foster past Secretary and player.

18 hole stroke play.

Don Hollingsworth Salver (1992)

Presented by the member.

Originally 18 hole stroke play for those over 60 years of age. Now a veterans' matchplay knock-out.

Master's Mug (1994)

Presented by ex-Captain Barry Brooks.

18 hole stroke play handicap played on the day of Trophy Presentation and therefore the final contest of the year. Contested by the winners of all competitions over the season.

Order of Merit (2001)

Points are accumulated over the year by those coming in the top ten of each competition with double points for the 'Majors'. Winner is obviously the player with the most points.

Mixed Trophies

Challenge Mixed Foursomes (1930)

Presented by the retiring captain AH Clarke.

A mixed foursomes knock-out.

Arthur Lock Rose Bowl (1947)

Presented by the family of past Captain Arthur Lock. It bears the touching inscription: *Presented in fulfillment of his wishes and in appreciation of so many happy days spent at Eaton by Mrs Arthur Lock and her sons Hugh and Peter.*

A singles mixed knock-out played through the summer.

Pettingill Salvers (1962)

Presented by Mrs Charles Pettingill in memory of her husband who was a member of both Eaton and Royal Norwich. He died on the 6th tee at Sheringham whilst playing for Norfolk.

An 18 hole stableford mixed foursomes open to members of both clubs and played for annually; the venue alternating between the two courses.

Freehold Trophy (1994)

A Florida scramble open to all members of the club in any combination. A replica of the British Open Claret Jug is played for in celebration of the purchase of the course on or nearest the date of completion.

Dr El Watson Memorial Trophy (2010)

A new trophy to celebrate the Club Centenary. In memory of the first Club Captain.

A stableford competition open to all members.

The elephant appears on the village sign for Eaton.

Ladies Trophies

Davidson-Walker Cup (1912)

Presented by Mrs Margaret Davidson-Walker, first Lady Captain and Lady President (1914-20).

For the best scratch score, Silver Division, over 36 holes in the Spring Event and the associated Medal.

Eaton Ladies Cup (1912)

Presented by the Club.

A match play competition for the winners of Monthly Medals (Silver and Bronze divisions).

Ladies Trophies

Charles Bunting Cup (1920)

Presented by Charles Bunting (Bunting's department store in London Street is now Habitat). Mrs Bunting was Lady Captain in 1921.

For the best net score in Medals 1 November to 31 October, Closed Meeting and Spring Event. Handicap limit 24.

Walter Bunting Cup (1926)

Presented by Mrs Walter Bunting, Lady Captain 1927, President 1926-38.

For the best net score, Bronze division, returned over 36 holes in the Spring Event and associated Medal.

Varnon Handicap Cup (1928)

Presented by Mrs C Varnon.

For the best net score, Silver Division, returned over 36 holes in the Spring Event and associated medal.

Ladies Scratch Cup (1928)

Bought by the Club.

For the best gross score, Bronze Division, over 36 holes in the Spring Event and associated medal.

Mrs WE Keefe Cup (1930)

Presented by Mrs WE Keefe, Lady Captain 1926, Lady President 1939-44.

Matchplay knockout for handicaps up to 24.

Mrs Keefe was desirous of presenting a challenge cup on her retirement from the Club after 20 years membership.

Mrs Russell Price Salver (1932)

Donated by Mrs Russell Price, Lady Captain 1931.

For the best gross score, Silver Division, over 36 holes in the Closed Meeting.

A windy spring day on the 3rd fairway, 1985.

Hines Junior Girls Cup (1934)

Presented by Mrs EE Hines, Lady President 1933–42.

A strokeplay competition, over 18 holes, played for on the third Sunday in September.

Pordage Cup (1934)

Presented by Mrs EJW Pordage, Lady President 1966–68.

For the greatest reduction in handicap November to October for intermediate and adult lady members.

Mrs McEwen Smith Salver (1934)

Presented by Mrs McEwen Smith, Lady Captain 1925.

For the best gross score over 36 holes in the Closed Meeting.

Gowing Cups Silver and Bronze (1937)

Presented by Mrs CT Gowing, Lady Captain, 1932–39.

For the best net scores over 36 holes in the Closed Meeting.

Bousfield Trophy (1948)

Presented by Miss G Bousfield (later Mrs G Rampling), Lady Captain 1946–47 and 1953, Lady President 1970–72, County President 1984, Life Member of Eaton 1982 and of NCLGA 1990.

A knockout competition for Business Ladies – if fewer than eight entries it is given to the lady with the best four medal scores January to December.

Neville Coe Salvers (1951)

Presented by Mrs Joyce Coe, Lady Captain 1952, Lady President 1974-76.

Knockout foursomes for high and low handicap pairs (drawn).

Mrs P Myhill Trophy (1953)

Presented by Mrs P Myhill, Lady Captain 1954.

Winter American Tournament (knockout competition played for by the winners of the drawn leagues).

Mrs AJG Spencer Cup (1960)

Presented by Mrs Betty Spencer, Lady Captain 1959, Lady President 1966-68.

For most points scored medals, stablefords, bogeys, first round of the Closed Meeting and the Thursday Medal round of the Spring Event.

2nd hole, today. The only hole that has survived unchanged from the very start.

Pordage Vase (Veterans' Cup) (1960)

Presented by
Mrs E J W Pordage.

Matchplay competition for Ladies aged 60+ on 1 January.

Mrs Glyn-Jones Vase (1961)

Presented by
Mrs Belle Glyn-Jones, Lady Captain 1961.

Matchplay competition for handicaps 21–32.

Past and Present Captains' Bowl (1962)

Presented by Mrs EG Cooper, Lady Captain 1962 and Lady President 1978–80.

For the Lady Captain of Eaton who returned the best score in the first round of the Closed Meeting.

Rampies Foursomes Salvers (1971)

Presented by Mr HG Rampling in memory of his wife 'Rampie', Lady Captain 1950 and President 1970–72.

18 hole Stableford.

President's Bowl (1972)

Crystal bowl presented by Mrs Grace Rampling, Lady Captain 1946–47 and President 1970–72.

Awarded on Lady President's Day – format decided by the Lady President.

Woolgar Granny Bowl (1975)

Presented by Mrs Monica Woolgar to the grandmother with the best nett score in the October Medal.

Dorothy Morgan Trophies Silver and Bronze (1978)

Presented by Miss D Morgan, Lady Captain 1928. She bequeathed to the Eaton Ladies' Section all her golfing trophies and replicas 'for such purposes as the committee may decide' in April 1977. Two small salvers were retained and re-engraved.

For the best four nett monthly Medal scores November to October inclusive.

Birdie Trophy (1980)

Presented by CH (Jock) Munro, Captain 1980.

His wife, Val, has been Lady Captain and President and County President (2003–04).

For the most birdies scored in Medals March–October.

Joyce Coe Memorial Trophies Silver and Bronze (1981)

Presented by her family. Lady Captain 1952, President 1974–76. Member for 60 years.

For the best nett scores in September Medal.

Kelly Vase (1981)

Presented by Bert Kelly in celebration of his 50 years as Professional with the Club.

Best score in the June Stableford.

Walter Bloom Trophy (1982)

Presented by Wally Bloom for the best aggregate score in the two Par competitions.

(July and August).

The Gainsford Cup (1982)

Presented by Mrs Peter Gainsford.

For the greatest reduction in handicap by a Junior girl.

Owl Trophy (1984)

Presented by Mrs J Lister when she was Lady Secretary (Captain 1998).

For the Junior girl who has returned the most cards in the year's competitions.

Captain's Cup (1989)

Presented by Mrs Ruth Gamble in her year of captaincy. To be played for on Lady Captain's Day to a format decided by the Lady Captain.

Mrs Ethel Wilson Cup (1990)

Presented by her son, Mr R (Bob) Perry, Club President, in her memory.

Best nett score in Bronze B Division in June Medal.

80th Anniversary Trophy (1991)

Presented by Mrs J O'Riordan, Lady Captain 1966, Lady President 1991–92 to mark the 80th Anniversary of Eaton Ladies' section.

Best nett score in November Medal.

Professional's Trophy (1992)

Presented by Frank Hill on his last Professional's Day.

To be played for in the October Stableford.

Edna Hollingsworth Trophy (1993)

Presented by
Mrs E Hollingsworth,
Lady Captain 1968 and
President 1984–86.

Awarded to the lady returning the best nett score in the May medal.

Ladies Club Championship Trophy (1993)

Presented by Mrs J Lee following her year of captaincy.

The four ladies returning the best gross scores in the Closed Meeting (36 holes) play in a knockout competition the next day to determine the Ladies Champion for that year.

Mary Cooper Spoons (1995)

Presented by Nick and Lottie Cooper in memory of Nick's mother.

For the best nett scores in Silver, Bronze A and Bronze B in the August medal.

Cook Trophy (2001)

Presented by Mrs Pauline Cook after her year of captaincy.

A matchplay competition for ladies handicap 29 to 36.

Lyn Black Clocks (2001)

Presented by Mrs Lyn Black, Lady Captain 1986 and President 2005–6.

A Texas Scramble.

Daisy Putter (2007)

Presented by Mrs Deidre Cursons in her year of Captaincy to the Lady with the fewest putts over four Medal rounds over the year.

Junior Trophies

Ward Cup (1926)

Presented by AW Ward and for many years the only, and still the premier, junior trophy.

18 hole stroke play under handicap.

Faulkener Cup (1971)

18 hole medal.

Ivor Dunnell Cup (1975)

Presented by the then Junior Organiser.

18 hole stroke play.

Top: Geoff Swain, World Trick-shot Champion at Eaton Golf Club.

Mike Quinton Shield (1977)

Presented by past Captain, President and the first Junior Organiser.

Won by the player with the best scratch score in the Junior competitions.

Nan Holloway Cup (1985)

Presented by Junior Co-organiser Mrs Nan Holloway who over
13 years devoted herself to the promotion of Junior golf at Eaton.

Jack Dunnell Family Foursomes(1985)

Presented by Junior Organiser.

Knockout Foursomes played by any Adult/Junior combination.

Club Championship Junior Handicap (1989)

Played in conjunction with Men's Club Championship.

Presidents Cup (1992)

18 hole medal.

Rampies Junior Open (1994)

Presented by Grace Rampling – past Lady President and Captain and a member since 1920.

Awarded to the junior member who records the highest position in the Eaton Junior Open.

Our Environment

We all consider ourselves fortunate to be able to play our golf in such delightful surroundings so close to the city centre. We should equally appreciate what an important feature of the local environment our course represents. It is our duty to protect and enhance this asset for generations to come.

With this in mind the club was very lucky when, in 2004, Head Greenkeeper Mick Lathrope won a free ecological survey of the course sponsored by the English Golf Union and English Nature.

Lee Penrose, the visiting ecologist, observes in his preface that

> *Eaton golf course not only provides an attractive and varied setting for golf, but equally supports considerable ecological and landscape interest. The features that enthuse and stimulate golfing interest also provide valuable habitat for wildlife.*

Geologically, the area occupied by the course can be conveniently split in two. The 'upper part' is typical heathland – a light, sandy soil on a substratum of chalk. The 'lower' holes are located

Head Greenkeeper since 1972, Mick Lathrope.

The course supports a significant population of muntjac.

in the flood plain of the River Yare, which flows some 400 metres south of the course boundary. The land between the course and the river is designated a SSSI (Site of Special Scientific Interest).

As such, it is home to, among other bird species, heron, kingfishers, reed warblers, cormorants, kestrel, sparrowhawk and marsh harrier. I have also spotted a barn owl quartering the marsh on my early morning dog walks. Mammalian inhabitants include water vole, shrew, mink, fox and otter which have been sighted upstream at Keswick Mill. However the most notable feature is the presence of the very rare marsh orchid in the wetlands in late spring.

The indigenous vegetation of the first nine-hole course (restricted to the land above the valley) was predominantly gorse interspersed with birch

and pine trees. The richer soil of the valley was mostly open grassland with the occasional mature native trees, such as oak and beech.

Much of the mixed woodland, which now dominates our course, was planted over the years. The report mentions:

> *The 110 acre course is given hole separation and definition by extensive tracts of introduced woodland supporting a variety of species and also a few localised areas of deep rough grassland. I suspect most of us have visited most of it without ever giving it a passing thought!*

Those of us who keep our eyes open when playing will have seen pheasants, rabbits, foxes (who don't seem to have much effect on the 'bunny' population), and, most charmingly, muntjac deer. Grass snakes and even adders are occasionally spotted. This is in addition to the many native species of bird, whose lives have been enhanced thanks to the introduction of bird boxes strategically placed by members Tony Stanley and Roger Smith, both keen ornithologists.

The following pages illustrate the development of the course over the years from the 'original' nine holes to the current layout. The yardages and their relation to the par for the holes are difficult to translate into 'modern' terms since the criteria have changed significantly over the years with the development of equipment.

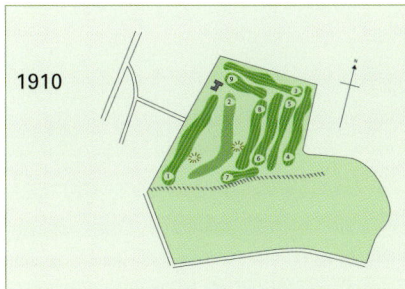

1910

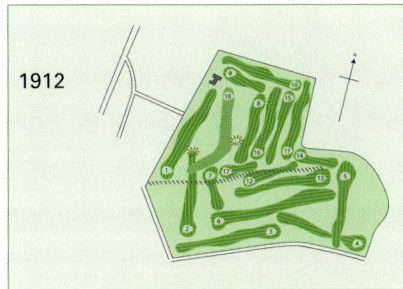

1912

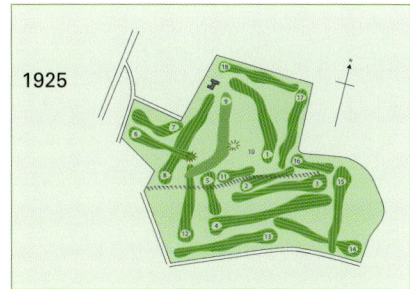

1925

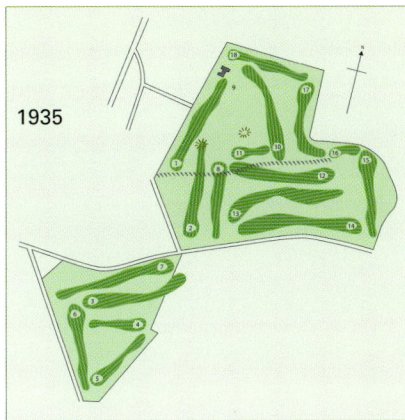

1935

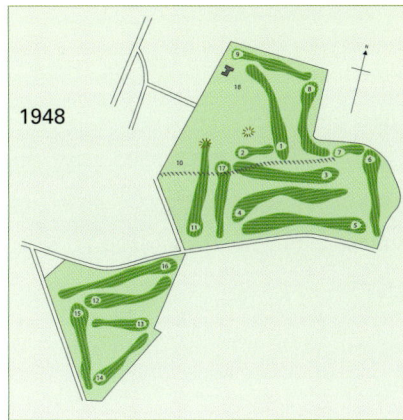

1948

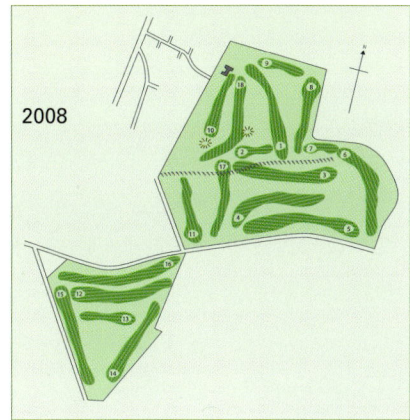

2008

Course layout 1910

designed by
Ernest Riseborough
(Sheringham).

It is worth noting that
there were very few
trees, the terrain being
open heathland with
gorse the predominant
vegetation. The 'bogey'
or par for these nine
holes was 40. The only
hole which remains
unchanged through the
generations is the 7th
(our 2nd) which can
therefore be considered
Eaton's signature hole.

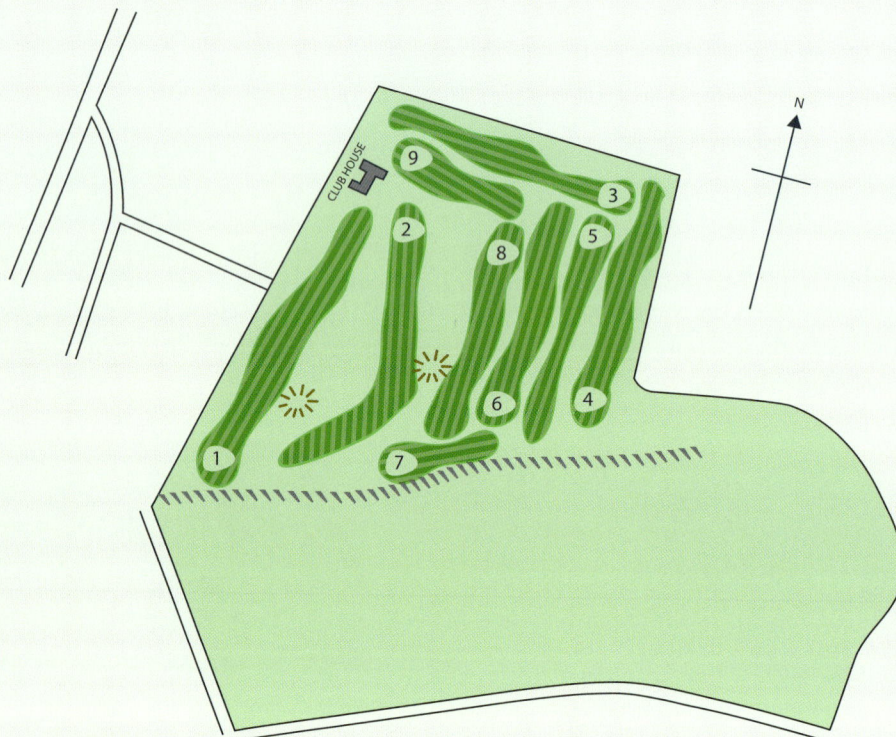

CLUB HOUSE

N

1	418 yds
2	409 yds
3	303 yds
4	308 yds
5	305 yds
6	285 yds
7	145 yds
8	330 yds
9	143 yds

Course layout 1912

designed by JH Taylor (five times Open Champion between 1898 and 1909).

This design extended the course to 18 holes using the newly acquired land below the escarpment. Our current 5th hole was divided into two holes (3 & 4) running from the proximity of the now 11th green into the far south-western corner where our 6th tee is located. Another feature was the 12th which was played over the levee from a tee near our 1st green to a green near the ladies' 3rd tee today.

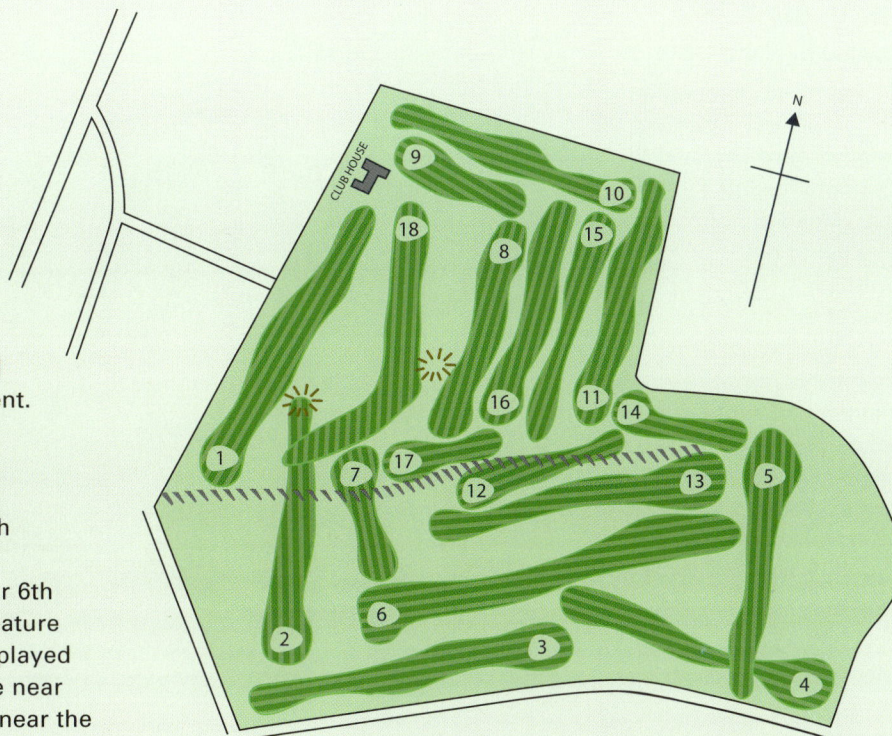

1	418 yds	**10**	305 yds
2	300 yds	**11**	305 yds
3	411 yds	**12**	220 yds
4	326 yds	**13**	412 yds
5	280 yds	**14**	190 yds
6	540 yds	**15**	385 yds
7	133 yds	**16**	285 yds
8	308 yds	**17**	145 yds
9	143 yds	**18**	409 yds

Course layout 1925

adapted by Sidney Gill.

In an attempt to lengthen the course and ease the congestion of Taylor's design, holes 6 & 7 were added on land to the west of our current site. This equates to the top part of Greenways between what is Fairways School (hence its name) and what was the Civil Service Sports ground. The thoroughfare on the extreme western boundary was known as Donkey Lane.

1	470 yds	**10**	405 yds
2	190 yds	**11**	120 yds
3	415 yds	**12**	330 yds
4	495 yds	**13**	415 yds
5	135 yds	**14**	340 yds
6	475 yds	**15**	320 yds
7	335 yds	**16**	190 yds
8	410 yds	**17**	350 yds
9	425 yds	**18**	315 yds

Course layout 1935

designed by Sidney Gill in consultation with Arthur Havers, Hellesdon (Open Champion 1923).

This layout, incorporating the land to the South of Marston Lane, represents the course much as we know it today save the reversal of the two nines. Soon after opening for play the 'new' holes were requisitioned for the planting of crops for the war effort. 18 holes were however maintained by playing 1, 2, 8 and 9 twice and by reverting to the two holes running parallel to Marston Lane as in 1923.

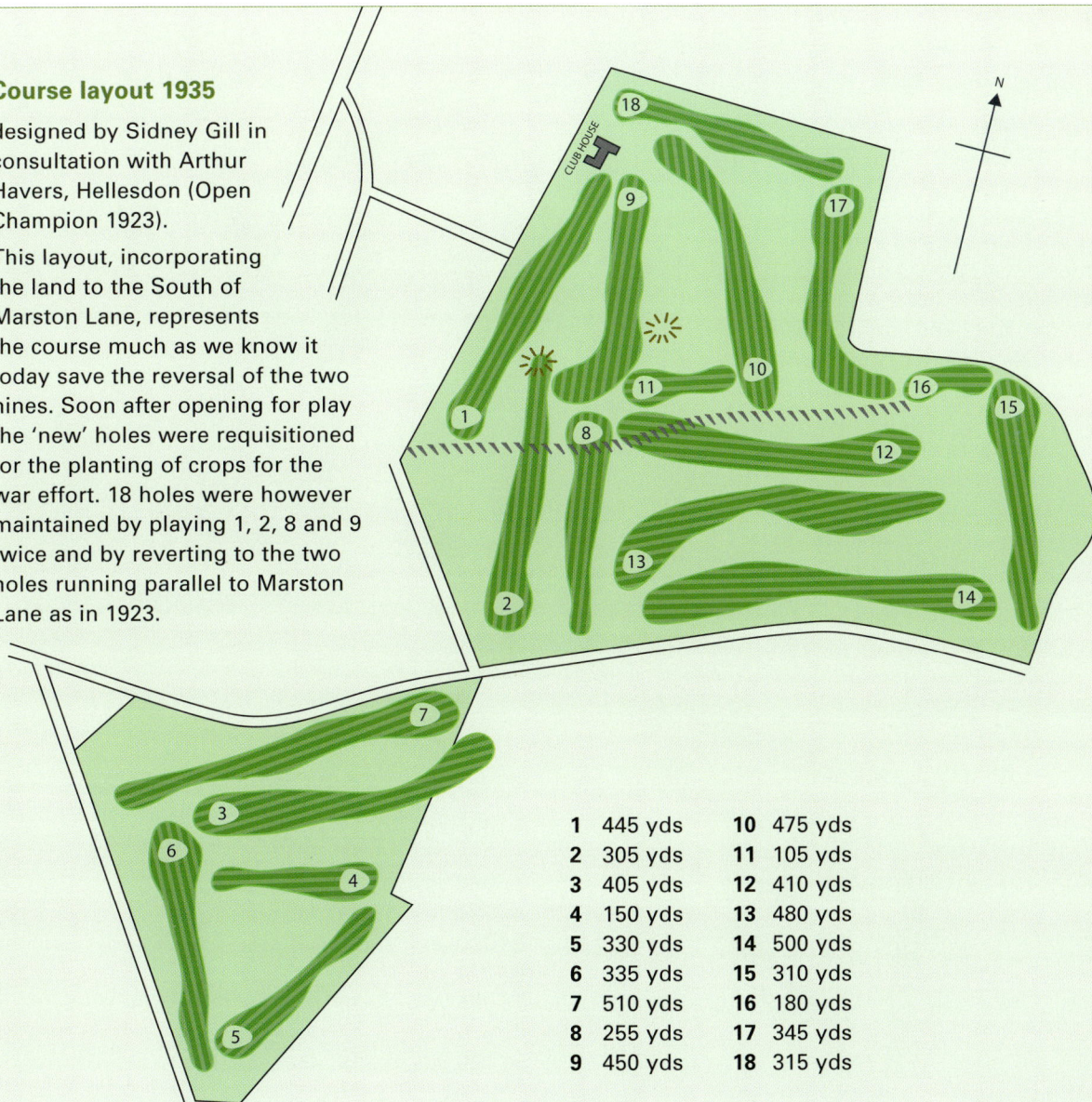

CLUB HOUSE

N

1	445 yds	**10**	475 yds
2	305 yds	**11**	105 yds
3	405 yds	**12**	410 yds
4	150 yds	**13**	480 yds
5	330 yds	**14**	500 yds
6	335 yds	**15**	310 yds
7	510 yds	**16**	180 yds
8	255 yds	**17**	345 yds
9	450 yds	**18**	315 yds

Course layout 1948

The configuration of the immediate post-war course would be most familiar to today's golfer; save the loop of holes 6, 7, 8 and 9. The 6th was played as a straight par 4 past the pit into the far right hand corner, the 7th was a short par 3 to the present 6th green and the 8th challenging par 4 dog-leg from the current 7th summer tee to our 8th green. The 9th was a straight par four from the current tee to a green approximately where our practice green is. It was also decided at this time to reverse the nines so the final hole finished in front of the clubhouse.

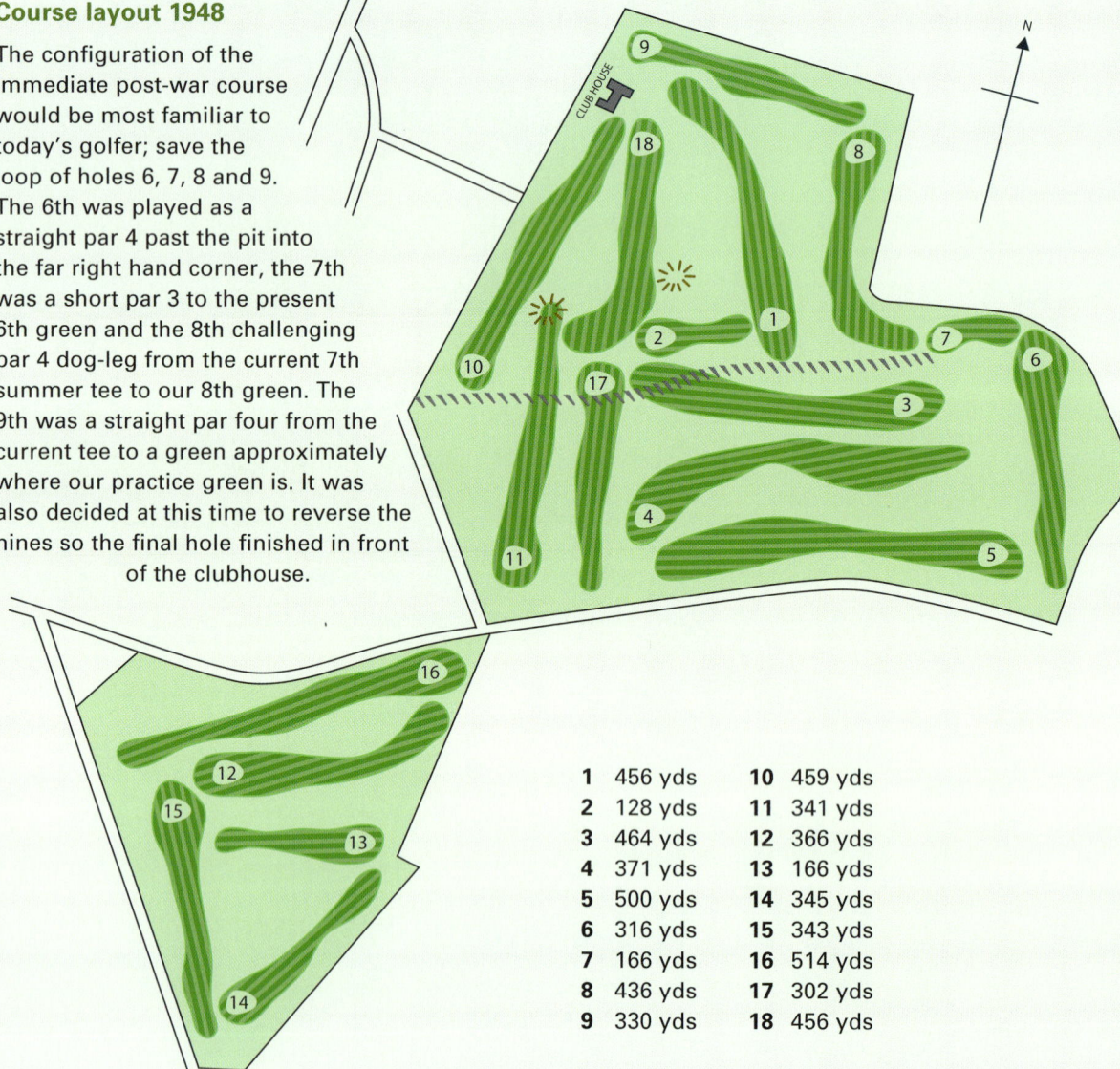

CLUB HOUSE

N

1	456 yds	**10**	459 yds
2	128 yds	**11**	341 yds
3	464 yds	**12**	366 yds
4	371 yds	**13**	166 yds
5	500 yds	**14**	345 yds
6	316 yds	**15**	343 yds
7	166 yds	**16**	514 yds
8	436 yds	**17**	302 yds
9	330 yds	**18**	456 yds

Course layout 2010

As mentioned in the text (page 45) most of the changes to the course since the 60s have been necessitated by the development of housing on our boundaries – notably holes 6, 7, 8, 9, 10 and 11. More recently we managed to swop a small tract of land behind the 14th green for the paddock behind the 5th green enabling the re-siting of the 6th tee thus lengthening the hole and tightening the drive.

In an attempt to make the links more of a challenge to the better player and to reflect the changes in modern equipment, a Course Architect, Simon Gidman, was commissioned in 2008. Most of his alterations involve the clearing of trees and scrub which present an unfair hazard to all players, especially the higher handicapper and the re-design of several bunkers to make the placement of the tee shot more critical. The work is a five year plan after which we hope that Eaton will not only present one of the sternest tests of inland golf in the region but also an enjoyable round for members and visitors of all abilities.

CLUB HOUSE

N

Hole	Yards	Hole	Yards
1	478 yds	10	361 yds
2	159 yds	11	163 yds
3	457 yds	12	352 yds
4	417 yds	13	161 yds
5	518 yds	14	350 yds
6	355 yds	15	336 yds
7	190 yds	16	510 yds
8	348 yds	17	301 yds
9	194 yds	18	468 yds

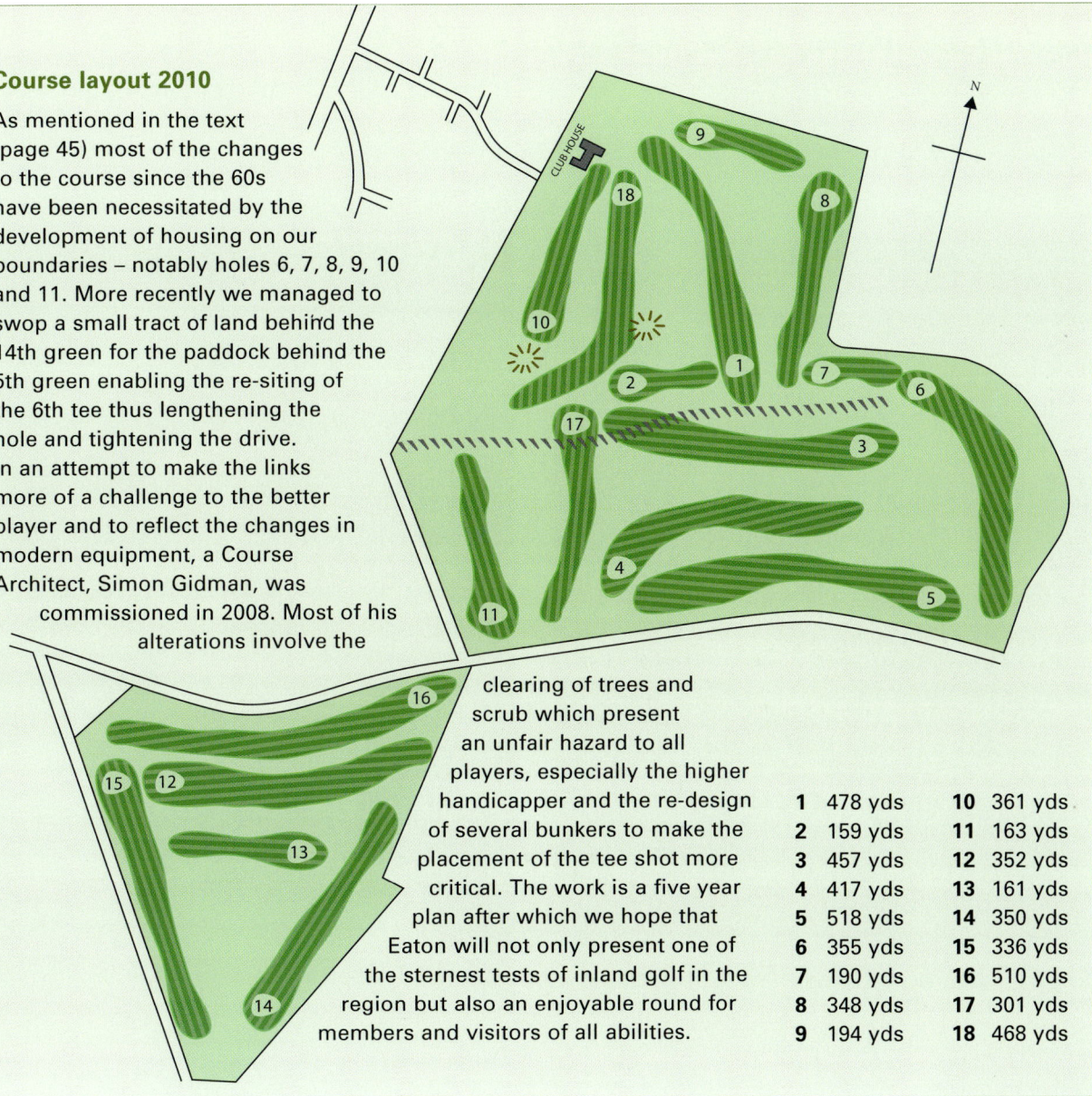

First Club Captain, Dr EI Watson
Captain 1911–12.

First Lady Captain, Mrs Davidson-Walker
Lady Captain 1911–14, President 1914–20.

Past Captains, Presidents and Chairmen

Past Captains

1911–12	Dr EI Watson
1913–14	Capt LE Gurney
1915–16	CT Coller
1917–18	WE Keefe
1919	AF Gentry
1920–22	EE Hines
1923	FW Morris
1924	SJ Wearing
1925–26	ST Gill
1927	HC Sampson
1928	RG Pilch
1929	JH Dain
1930–31	AH Clarke
1932–33	RB Keefe
1934	A Lock
1935	CF Page
1936	F Green
1937–38	PR Burroughes
1939	T Clay
1940	AC James
1941	RH Caldwell
1942–44	HA Towlson
1945	CC Amey
1946	HS Downes
1947	HA Towlson
1948	A Shingler
1949–50	AR Croskill
1951	W Robinson
1952	HS Cann
1953	CC Amey
1954	BW Brett
1955	FB Nichols
1956	TF Swift
1957	TJ McColl
1958	JJ Mc Innes
1959	N Hatch
1960	EA Rutherford
1961	DE Tryer
1962	AR Cobb
1963	FW Hull
1964	GB Menzies
1965	WT Freshwater
1966	KH Howard

Captain LE Gurney
Captain 1913–14

JH Dain, Captain 1929
Chief Constable.

1967	WAJ Spear	1989	JE Vallis
1968	NF Coe	1990	BM Noble
1969	E Yeeles	1991	DM Gibbs
1970	AM Unsworth	1992	MF Hull
1971	JFP Quinton	1993	DG Stewart
1972	RJ Perry Snr	1994	BJ Brooks
1973	WT Skinner	1995	CJ Lingwood
1974	GA Corke	1996	RM Fenn
1975	BJ Francis	1997	AD Nichols
1976	EM Sandland	1998	RS Moore
1977	GL Clarke	1999	JC Scotting
1978	GJ Gerrish	2000	TT Ferguson
1979	B King	2001	JM Cooke
1980	CH Munro	2002	MI Gaston
1981	PO Sheridan	2003	R Mcdonald
1982	DR Kearney	2004	CJ Gillham
1983	DP Lister	2005	AC Baker
1984	MG Quinton	2006	RG Harvey
1985	DC Chapman	2007	RJ Ong
1986	LJ Rowe	2008	AN Christie
1987	EJ Brister	2009	R Ball
1988	P White	2010	CS Brown

Presidents

1910–19	JH Gurney
1920–32	JH Colman
1933–42	EE Hines
1943–60	ST Gill
1961–62	AR Croskill
1963–64	T Clay
1965–66	CC Amey
1967–69	TF Swift
1970–71	FB Nicholls
1972–73	EA Rutherford
1974–75	NF Coe
1976	TJ McColl
1977–78	AJG Spencer
1979–80	HS Clay
1981–82	WS Palmer
1983–84	P Deavin
1985–86	EM Sandland
1987–88	J Phillips
1989	GL Clarke
1990–91	LJ Rowe
1992–93	RJ Perry Snr
1994–95	DC Chapman
1996–97	MG Quinton
1998–99	N Harrison OBE
2000	CH Munro
1996	EJ Brister
1997	DR Kearney
1998	P White
1999	D Lister
2009–10	MI Gaston

Stanley J Wearing, Captain 1924
Architect of the 1921 clubhouse.

Mrs Julia Amey
Lady Centenary President
Captain 1993
First Lady voted onto General
Committee.

Lady Captains

1911–14	Mrs M Davidson-Walker
1915	Miss D Adcock
1916–19	Miss I Bond
1920	Miss G Barnard
1921	Mrs C Bunting
1922–23	Miss I Bond
1924	Mrs E Deuchar
1925	Miss McEwan Smith
1926	Mrs W Keefe
1927	Mrs W Bunting
1928	Miss D Morgan
1929	Mrs RB Keefe
1930	Miss E Stimpson
1931	Mrs Russell Price
1932	Mrs CT Gowing
1933	Miss M Pilch
1934	Miss EK Harmer
1935	Mrs JA Clymer
1936	Miss E Stimpson
1937	Mrs AC Cooke
1938	Mrs WT George
1939	Mrs CT Gowing
1940–45	Mrs RB Keefe
1946–47	Miss G Bousfield
1948	Mrs HJ Harrison
1949	Mrs JH Martin
1950	Mrs HG Rampling
1951	Mrs WH Byron
1952	Mrs N Coe
1953	Mrs HG Rampling
1954	Mrs P Myhill
1955	Mrs AC Rose
1956	Miss NK Maingay
1957	Miss AC Rose
1958	Mrs H Willis
1959	Mrs LM Hodgson
1960	Mrs AJG Spencer
1961	Mrs FJ Moore
1962	Mrs S Glyn Jones
1963	Mrs EG Cooper
1964	Mrs GB Menzies
1965	Miss PA Brett
1966	Miss J O'Riordan

1967	Miss AM Eastoe	1989	Mrs S Chapman
1968	Mrs DS Hollingsworth	1990	Mrs L Harris
1969	Mrs N Hatch	1991	Mrs M Williams
1970	Mrs WF Cullington	1992	Miss J Lee
1971	Mrs J Trett	1993	Mrs JA Amey
1972	Mrs J Musgrave	1994	Mrs D Hull
1973	Mrs BJR Bell	1995	Mrs N Rowe
1974	Mrs HM Burn	1996	Miss GM Baker
1975	Mrs AW Goring	1997	Mrs E Clayton
1976	Mrs FS Tann	1998	Mrs J Lister
1977	Mrs P Deavin	1999	Mrs M Baker
1978	Mrs WS Palmer	2000	Mrs J Pank
1979	Mrs GJ Gerrish	2001	Mrs P Cook
1980	Mrs J Brister	2002	Mrs N Stewart
1981	Mrs V Munro	2003	Mrs B Gaston
1982	Mrs C Fisher	2004	Mrs S Ashford
1983	Mrs BA Rhodes	2005	Mrs M Jones
1984	Mrs J Palframan	2006	Miss S Wybar
1985	Mrs LM Bygrave	2007	Mrs D Cursons
1986	Mrs L Black	2008	Mrs A Stanley
1987	Mrs C Fuller	2009	Mrs J Knowler
1988	Mrs R Gamble	2010	Mrs C Jeffries

Mrs Val Munro, Captain 1981
President 1997–98
County Ladies President and Secretary.

Mrs MF Leist-Grimer
Lady President 1921–25.

Lady Presidents

1914–20	Mrs M Davidson-Walker
1921–25	Mrs Leist-Grimer
1926–38	Mrs W Bunting
1939–44	Mrs WE Keefe
1944–60	Mrs CW Hardesty
1960–62	Mrs HG Rampling
1962–64	Mrs AC Rose
1964–66	Mrs GM Brett
1966–68	Mrs EJW Pordage
1968–70	Mrs WH Byron
1970–72	Mrs G Rampling
1972–74	Mrs GB Menzies
1974–76	Mrs NF Coe
1976–78	Mrs AJG Spencer
1978–80	Mrs EG Cooper
1980–82	Miss IM Griffiths MBE
1982–84	Mrs BJR Bell
1984–86	Mrs DS Hollingsworth
1987–89	Mrs J Musgrave
1989–91	Mrs P Deavin
1991–93	Mrs J O'Riordan
1993–95	Mrs HM Burn
1995–96	Mrs J Brister
1997–99	Mrs V Munro
1999–2001	Mrs C Fisher
2001–2003	Mrs J Palframan
2003–2005	Mrs L Bygrave
2005–2007	Mrs L Black
2007–2009	Mrs S Chapman
2009–2011	Mrs J Amey

Chairmen

1995–2001	DC Chapman
2001–2003	JC Scotting
2003–2004	MI Gaston
2004–2007	R McDonald
2007–2010	MW Hart

Acknowledgements

A volume such as this is not just the work of the author but is dependent on the contributions of so many to whom I am greatly indebted.

As in the foreword I acknowledge the invaluable efforts of John Brister in compiling his history of the first 85 years. He has taken a keen interest in all I have done. I thank him in particular for his several proof readings, which have highlighted any factual inaccuracies.

The other person without whom this book would never have seen the light of day is Jennifer Hannaford, my book designer. We have spent hours and hours deciding on layout, revising text and poring over hundreds of pictures. Her professional skills and interest she has shown in the work have been an inspiration when my efforts were flagging. Thanks are also due to her husband, Michael for his help with digital photography.

We are also very grateful to William Colman and his staff at Colman Print for their help and advice pre-production. Similarly PS Digital Origination have been most useful with their scans of old photographs.

Two prominent members of the Club also deserve mention; Julia Amey, Centenary Lady President, for her research into the Lady players and Catherine Jeffries, Centenary Lady Captain for her work on the Ladies Trophies.

My thanks also go to, in no particular order: Andrew Cole (Graphic Designer) for the course plans, Eastern Counties Newspapers (Archant) Library for the use of their resources and permission to reproduce articles/pictures from their archive, The Royal and Ancient Golf Club of St Andrews for the picture of JH Taylor, Mike Trendell for various photos and Jayne Wilkinson for proof reading. I would like to acknowledge the late Richard Tilbrook for the many slides he left the Club.

I am also indebted to the office at Eaton GC for all their help and support (in particular Liz Bovill and Peter Johns) and the many members who have shown an interest in the compilation of this book.

Lastly I would like to thank the Board of Management and the Centenary Committee for entrusting me with the task and their support throughout.

Nigel Simpson

Calendar of the Year 2010

July

10th & 11th	*Dr EI Watson Memorial Trophy*
27th	*Ladies Centenary Stableford*

August

1st	*Men's County II v Northants*
14th	*Liberator Salver – Invited players from USAAF*
26th	*Norfolk Open*

September

12th	*Norfolk Centenary Clubs Cup*

October

9th	*Centenary Dinner – Top of the Terrace*

November

20th	*Wobbly Wine Evening*

December

Christmas Party
New Year's Eve Party

Here's to the next 100 years
PHOTO REPRODUCED WITH KIND PERMISSION OF PARENTS